PRAISE FOR BETA

As a Sunday School teacher for 20 years, Beta was the best received course that I have ever taught. Participants also stated that it was the best class they had ever attended and that everyone in the church needs to take this course.

JOHN FUGATE, M.D.
Christ Presbyterian Church
Edina, Minnesota

Note: The following comments are from participants in a Beta seminar. The number in the parentheses after each person's professional identification indicates how many years each has known the Lord.

This course has helped me in every possible way. It has been faith building, skill building and confidence building. I treasured both the teaching and the fellowship.
Retired counselor (4)

It helped me know that no one (not even my husband) can keep me from being the person God created me to be.
Homemaker and musician (40)

This course has lifted my burdens off my shoulders. I feel renewed. It was like the Lord has spoken to me, and consequently, I feel closer to Jesus.
Retired man (18)

I feel so much closer to Jesus and I have learned so many ways to show how much He loves me. I learned the best I can be is what He created me to be: a wife and mother and to raise my children to serve and love our Lord.
Homemaker (18)

It was eye opening and freeing. It put everything in perspective with tangible helps to know who I am in Christ and how to walk the walk in victory.
Homemaker and teacher (46)

It has helped me free up the past, so I can look to the future.
Homemaker (33)

The focus on the freedom we have in Christ helped bring a new dimension to my faith.
Business executive (3)

It helped me realize and gave me the tools to let go of the baggage I was still carrying around after all these years.
Homemaker (8)

I understood my Christian life more clearly and realized how things in my life should change; I should change.
Salesperson (50)

It renewed my faith, restored a positive thought process, restored God to His proper place in my life and restored a sense of significance that has been missing lately.
Retired computer programmer (8)

It helped me get back my first love for Christ. It also helped me remember where I've come from and reaffirm my faith.
Service manager (30)

It really boosted and refreshed my walk with Christ, helped me understand the battle for my mind and emotions and confirmed to me who I am in Christ.
College student (8)

The course reinforced biblical truths and helped me face some sin in my life.
Homemaker (50)

I feel more focused on Jesus and the impact He can have on my life if I let Him.
Homemaker (23)

It returned my focus to share my faith more, to pray for opportunities, to rely on Jesus more and to speak boldly in freedom.
Teacher (49)

This course reaffirmed that God loves me. I don't have to carry this baggage around. I'm a new person who is free and I hope—no, I pray—I can serve the Lord Jesus Christ.
Homemaker and bookkeeper (3)

It has grounded my faith in Christ and illuminated the truths and revealed my misconceptions about my walk with Him.
Real estate broker (10)

I believe it has given me a new perspective and hopefully tools to do away with my past.
Business broker (37)

It was a great foundation for who I am in Christ, and I am excited to dig deeper.
Teacher (6)

It has helped me understand and appropriate who I am in Christ and understand what that means. I am renewed.
Teacher (15)

Wonderful foundation for who I am in Christ.
Marketing executive (33)

There was so much excellent insight and reinforcement of truth said in such a clearly understandable way.
Child-care worker (21)

It expanded my vision of God's kingdom—my part in it—and reaffirmed to me how important wholeness in Jesus is.
Interior designer (10)

I have been very blessed. This course has given me such incredible insight into some of the things I face, and the Lord showed me some things in my life that He wants to minister to me. I found freedom in significant places.
Graphic designer and Christian counselor (26)

LEADER'S GUIDE

beta

A LIFE-CHANGING
DISCIPLESHIP PROGRAM FROM

NEIL T. ANDERSON

 Gospel Light

Gospel Light is a Christian publisher dedicated to serving the local church. We believe God's vision for Gospel Light is to provide church leaders with biblical, user-friendly materials that will help them evangelize, disciple and minister to children, youth and families.

It is our prayer that this Gospel Light resource will help you discover biblical truth for your own life and help you minister to others. May God richly bless you.

For a free catalog of resources from Gospel Light, please call your Christian supplier or contact us at 1-800-4-GOSPEL *or* www.gospellight.com.

PUBLISHING STAFF

William T. Greig, Chairman

Bill Greig III, Publisher

Dr. Elmer L. Towns, Senior Consulting Publisher

Natalie Clark, Product Line Manager

Pam Weston, Managing Editor

Patti Pennington Virtue, Associate Editor

Hilary Young, Editorial Assistant

Jessie Minassian, Editorial Assistant

Bayard Taylor, M.Div., Senior Editor, Biblical and Theological Issues

Rob Williams, Cover

Zelle Olson, Internal Designer

ISBN 0-8307-3017-6

CONTENTS

INTRODUCTION

Jesus commanded us to "go therefore and make disciples" (Matthew 28:19). While effective evangelism has produced many *converts*, many are not firmly rooted in Christ, and because of this they struggle with their Christian walk. We need to take the next step and develop reproducing *disciples*.

Jesus said, "You will know the truth, and the truth will make you free" (John 8:32). Some don't know the truth and are perishing for their lack of knowledge (see Hosea 4:6). Paul wanted to give the church at Corinth solid food, but he could only give them milk because they "were not able to receive it" (1 Corinthians 3:2). "Jealousy and strife" (v. 3) prevented them from receiving the truth in a life-transforming way. Truth without repentance is stagnation. Although there are excellent discipleship programs and resources, Christians must also have the tools to connect with God and to appropriate biblical truth into their daily lives.

The Beta discipleship course is designed to communicate the essential truths of the Christian faith. Understanding these truths will help all believers—from new converts to those who need to renew their walk—resolve personal and spiritual conflicts through genuine repentance.

Note: The DVD for the Beta course features video presentations of each lesson by Dr. Neil Anderson. It is recommended that each participant have his or her own copy of the Beta Student Guide, which contains outlines of each session along with discussion questions and application helps.

COURSE GOALS

This course will enable you to

- Explain creation, the Fall and the gospel in such a way that believers can truly connect with their heavenly Father and integrate the life of Jesus Christ into their daily lives;
- Explain and help believers understand the nature of the spiritual battle for their minds and equip them to overcome the temptations of the world, the flesh and the devil;

- Illustrate how mental strongholds are developed and how they can be torn down through relationship with Jesus Christ;
- Instruct believers in becoming mentally and emotionally free from the past through the process of forgiving others;
- Lead believers to genuine repentance in a kind and gentle way;
- Equip believers to keep living by faith in the power of the Holy Spirit, so they can mature and bear fruit;
- Encourage believers to relate to one another in a godly way; and
- Start believers on the path of renewing their mind and being sanctified.

LEADER PREPARATION

If you are going to lead a course designed to help other Christians live in freedom and grow in Christ, you first need a good understanding of what it means to be alive and free in Christ yourself.

Familiarize Yourself with What You Are Teaching

It would be very beneficial for you to read both *Victory over the Darkness*[1] and *The Bondage Breaker*[2] before teaching this course. However, if you cannot do this, it is very important that you read through each session of this course and complete the Steps to Freedom in Christ (the Steps) yourself.[3]

Complete the Steps to Freedom in Christ (the Steps)

Completing the Steps is a two-hour process during which you invite the Holy Spirit to show you areas of your life that need to be dealt with in order to experience your own freedom in Christ. (It could take much longer for difficult counseling cases. The book *Discipleship Counseling* explains in depth the theology and methodology for the Steps.)[4]

Most mature Christians can process the Steps on their own; however, many have profited greatly by having a trained encourager take them through the process. Ideally, this is something that you would go through in your own church. If that is not possible, Freedom in Christ Ministries can assist you in finding a local representative or church that can serve you in this way. Visit us on the web at www.ficm.org or contact us at (865) 342-4000 for more information.

DIFFERENT TEACHING SETTINGS

Once your church has used the Beta course to train every member with the principles of living free in Christ, the course can become part of your training for new Christians and new members. The material is designed to be flexible enough to use in a variety of church situations.

In Combination with the Alpha Course

This course can be combined successfully with the Alpha course, Bible studies designed for not-yet Christians.[5] You could bring together Alpha participants and participants in this course for a meal and fellowship time each week and then dismiss participants to their designated classes after the meal.

Systematic Teaching with Small-Group Follow-Up

The message portion of each session is approximately 30 minutes long and can be used in your main church teaching program with weekly small-group meetings for in-depth follow-up.

Cell Groups

This course is excellent for use in cell groups. Each session follows the four-W format: Welcome, Worship, Word and Witness. The main focus of each session is the Word section; however, all four Ws are important. If 12 message-intensive sessions in a row seems a bit too much for your group, consider adding more sessions, rather than reducing the content so that the Welcome, Worship and Witness elements are not excluded from the program.

Midweek Church Meetings

You can use this course in your midweek church meeting by presenting the message to everyone gathered and then dividing into small groups for discussion.

SESSION STRUCTURE

Each session in the Beta course is designed with the following elements:

Session Overview

The session overview contains notes for the leader, including the focus verse, the objectives of the session, the focus truth and a briefing of the session.

Welcome

During this first part of each session, you will present participants with an opening question, story or illustration designed to help them relate to each other and also to the theme of the message.

Worship

Although music is a wonderful way to worship the Lord, it is not the only way. Worship can be done through playing music and singing, praying, praising, sharing testimonies or a combination of any of these elements.

Word

Communicating the message is the main part of each session and can be done either by viewing the presentation by Dr. Anderson on the *Beta DVD* or by presenting the message yourself from this course book. Whichever method you choose, the presentation will last approximately 30 minutes. Keep in mind that participants will have an outline of the message in their student guides with room for note taking, along with salient points and interactive questions. We've included tips in the Word section to help make the session more interactive. These tips are called Pause for Thoughts.

- **Presenting the Message Yourself:** If you are presenting the message of each session yourself, study thoroughly the Word section of each session. Be mindful of the outline in the student guide, and be sure to cover all the material so that participants can discuss all the study questions.
- **Using the *Beta DVD*:** If you are using the DVD presentation, simply start it at the end of your worship time. Do not neglect the Welcome

activity as the DVD will often refer to something done during the welcome time.

As you watch the *Beta DVD*, you will notice that the video does not perfectly match the *Beta Student Guide* outline. This is due to the fact that the printed materials were developed first and the student guide matches the *Beta Leader's Guide*. In the interest of time Dr. Anderson's presentation of each session is not as lengthy as the information available in the leader's guide, but the DVD does provide the essential information needed to understand and discuss the concepts of each session.

Note: Plan a group outing or special meeting to take place between sessions 9 and 10 so that you can lead participants through the Steps to Freedom in Christ as presented in their student guides—and also in this course guide on pages 80-106.

Witness

The witness element of the session contains a question or encouragement to help participants relate what has been learned to a strategy for reaching out to those who are not yet Christians.

Group Discussion Questions

During this segment of the session, participants will form small groups to discuss questions that will help them apply the message of the session in practical ways.

Taking It with You

This is the final segment of each session and includes a suggestion for quiet times during the coming week and a thought-provoking question to consider before the next session.

A FINAL WORD FROM DR. NEIL T. ANDERSON

The objective of Freedom in Christ Ministries is to equip Christian leaders to help people live in freedom and grow in Christ. If the material raises theological questions for you, in addition to *Victory over the Darkness* and *The Bondage Breaker*, let me encourage you to read *God's Power at Work in You*, which I coauthored with Dr. Robert Saucy.[6] This book covers the doctrine of sanctification in depth.

If you feel uncomfortable or unqualified leading your group through the Steps, the DVD has an interactive video that can be used to take the participants through the process. When you take participants through the Steps, some participants may not be able to process the Steps on their own in a group setting in the amount of time given. The bonus session has instruction for how to facilitate individual appointments. For more information to prepare you on helping participants individually, you would profit greatly by reading *Discipleship Counseling*.

Notes
1. Neil T. Anderson, *Victory over the Darkness*, rev. ed. (Ventura, CA: Regal Books, 2000).
2. Neil T. Anderson, *The Bondage Breaker* (Eugene, OR: Harvest House, 2000).
3. Neil T. Anderson, T*he Steps to Freedom in Christ* (Ventura, CA: Gospel Light, 2001).
4. Neil T. Anderson, *Discipleship Counseling* (Ventura, CA: Regal Books, 2003).
5. For more information on Alpha courses, visit www.alphacourse.org.
6. Neil T. Anderson and Robert L. Saucy, *God's Power at Work in You* (Eugene, OR: Harvest House, 2001).

THE GOOD NEWS

HE WHO HAS THE SON HAS THE LIFE; HE WHO DOES NOT
HAVE THE SON OF GOD DOES NOT HAVE THE LIFE.
1 JOHN 5:12

SESSION OVERVIEW

OBJECTIVE

In this session, you will help participants understand how Adam and Eve's sin resulted in their descendants being separated from God and that Jesus came, not only to give us life, but also to meet our needs for eternal life, identity, acceptance, security and significance.

FOCUS TRUTH

Before we became Christians we were born physically alive but spiritually dead—separated from God—with needs that cannot be fulfilled by human effort. In Christ, we are spiritually alive children of God who are accepted, secure and significant.

BRIEFING

Who am I? On the surface, this may seem like an easy question to answer; however, the way in which Christians respond to the question reveals what they believe about the gospel and their spiritual heritage.

Christians must understand why their needs for identity, acceptance, security and significance cannot be fully met through appearance, performance and social status. In this first session, you will help prepare participants to understand the whole gospel, including how their needs are met by becoming children of God. (This will be continued in session 2.)

THE GOOD NEWS

HE WHO HAS THE SON HAS THE LIFE; HE WHO DOES NOT
HAVE THE SON OF GOD DOES NOT HAVE THE LIFE.
1 JOHN 5:12

WELCOME

Welcome participants and begin the meeting in prayer, asking God to guide each person there into a deeper relationship with Him and thanking Him for sending His Son, Jesus, so that we can have eternal life with Him.

Pair up each participant with someone he or she does not know well, and allow two minutes for partners to find out as much as they can about one another. Then give participants 30 seconds each to tell the group as much as they can about their partners.

WORSHIP

Spend a few minutes worshiping the Lord through prayer, song, praise or testimonies shared by volunteers.

WORD

 The Word section is available on the Beta DVD, or you can present the information yourself in a lecture format.

THE GOOD NEWS

Read the following illustration from *Glad to Be Me: Building Self-Esteem in Yourself and Others*:

Have you ever thought about who you really are and why you were born? Are you just a physical being who makes a living, hoping for a little pleasure in life, then dies? Are you the person you pretend to be? If others got to know the real you, would they like you? Perhaps the following expresses how you feel:

Don't be fooled by me. Don't be fooled by the face I wear. I wear a mask. I wear a thousand masks—masks that I am afraid to take off, and none of them are me.

Pretending is an art that is second nature to me, but don't be fooled. For my sake, don't be fooled. I give the impression that I am secure, that all is sunny and unruffled within me as well as without, that confidence is my name and coolness my game; that the water is calm and I am in command, and that I need no one. But don't believe me, please. My surface may seem smooth, but my surface is my mask, my ever-varying and ever-concealing mask.

Beneath lies no smugness, no compliance. Beneath dwells the real me in confusion, in fear, in aloneness. I hide that. I don't want anybody to know it. I panic at the thought of my weakness and fear being exposed. That's why I frantically create a mask to hide behind—nonchalant, sophisticated façade—to help me pretend, to shield me from the glance that knows. But such a glance is precisely my salvation, my only salvation, and I know it. That is, it's followed by acceptance if it's followed by love.

It's the only thing that can liberate me from myself, from my own self-built prison wall, from the barriers I so painstakingly erect. It's the only thing that will assure me of what I can't assure myself—that I am really something . . .

"Who am I?" You may wonder. I am someone you know very well. I am every man you meet. I am every woman you meet. I am every child you meet. I am right in front of you. Please—love me![1]

Continue by sharing the following information about the creation of humankind.

CREATED IN THE IMAGE OF GOD

Each of us has worn a mask at one time or another, probably because we've felt the sting of rejection, insecurity and insignificance. Although we struggle for acceptance, security and significance, this was not how God created us to live in the beginning. Both Adam and Eve were created in the image of God (see Genesis 1:26-27).

"The LORD God formed man of dust from the ground, and breathed into his nostrils the breath of life; and man became a living being" (Genesis 2:7). When Adam was created by God, he was alive in two ways. First, he was alive physically: His soul was in union with his physical body. Second, he was alive spiritually: His soul was in union with God. When God created Eve as a companion for Adam (see Genesis 2:18), her soul was in union with her body and also with God.

Being intimately connected to God gave Adam and Eve purpose and meaning in life. Adam and Eve both knew that they were

- **Significant**—Adam and Eve did not have to search for significance or meaning in life; they already knew why they had been created. Their divine purpose for being on Earth was to rule over the beasts of the field and the fish of the sea (see Genesis 1:26).
- **Safe**—Adam and Eve had absolutely everything they needed, and in fact, neither had any concept of what it meant to need anything. They were safe and secure in God's presence.
- **Accepted**—Adam and Eve were in perfect communion with God. Both had a sense of belonging to Him as well as to each other. They were naked and unashamed—after all, they had nothing to hide. Even their intimate sexual relationship with each other was pure in the presence of God because sexual urges were in harmony with God's will—as was all of nature.

Pause for Thought
Imagine Adam and Eve's daily life before the Fall. How would it have been different from your daily life? What thoughts might have crossed the minds of Adam and Eve as they drifted off to sleep each night?

THE CONSEQUENCES OF THE FALL

When Adam and Eve gave in to the temptation to eat from the one tree from which they had been forbidden to eat, their sin had far-reaching results.

Spiritual Death

While Adam and Eve didn't die physically right after eating from the forbidden tree, they did die spiritually (see Genesis 2:16-17). As a consequence, every descendant of Adam is born into this world physically alive but spiritually dead (see Romans 5:12; 1 Corinthians 15:21-22).

Jesus came to remove the separation caused by Adam and Eve. Before coming to Christ, we have neither the presence of God in our lives nor the knowledge of His ways. From birth we live independently of God, separated from Him. When we accept Christ, we become alive in Him and our souls are united with God.

Mental Depravity

Before the Fall, Adam had no need to search for significance. There was no emptiness in his heart because he was without sin—and consciously in the presence of God. He knew his purpose.

When the wisdom of God was no longer within Adam and Eve, they hopelessly struggled to find their identity, their purpose and the meaning for their lives apart from their creator. The fact that Adam was deficient in his understanding became evident when he tried to hide from an omnipresent God (see Genesis 3:7-8).

Paul described Adam's descendants as "being darkened in their understanding, *excluded from the life of God* because of the ignorance that is in them, because of the hardness of their heart" (Ephesians 4:18, emphasis added). Before accepting Christ, we are darkened in our understanding because we do not have the life of Christ within us. Paul also wrote that the natural person who is spiritually dead cannot discern the things of God because such things are spiritually discerned (see 1 Corinthians 2:14). In such a state we can know *about* God, but we can't really know Him until we establish a relationship with Him through Jesus Christ.

Emotional Depravity

- **They felt fearful and anxious.** The first emotion expressed by Adam was in Genesis 3:10 when he said, "I was afraid." Many times throughout the Bible, the phrase "do not fear" can be found. It is hard to imagine that Adam and Eve had no irrational fears until they sinned, but it's true. Today anxiety disorders are the number one mental-health problem in the world.

- **They felt guilty and ashamed.** When their relationship with God was broken, it was replaced by a sense of guilt and shame. As a result, Adam and Eve longed for some sense of worth. What had belonged to them before their sin now became a glaring need.

- **They felt depressed and angry.** Before the Fall, Adam and Eve had only one bad choice they could make: to eat from the forbidden tree. Other than that, they could make no bad choices. After the Fall, they were bombarded with choices, both good and bad. Overwhelmed, they became depressed and angry. Today, depression is the common cold of mental illness, and despite modern technological advances, the whole world continues to experience a blues epidemic in an age of anxiety.

- **They felt powerless.** When they were created, Adam and Eve had the power of God within them, allowing them to be and to do all that He created them to be and to do. After they sinned, they had to rely on their own strength and resources. As a result, they tried to control their own destiny apart from God, and the power they desperately sought failed them.

- **They felt rejected.** The loss of their relationship with God resulted in a crushing sense of rejection for Adam and Eve—and their descendants. Trying to gain the acceptance of others through appearance, performance and social status has proven to be elusive. There is no way we can humanly give or receive unconditional love and acceptance. The best of human effort eventually results in personal rejection, hostile criticism and morbid introspection.

Pause for Thought
Which of the feelings—fear, anxiety, guilt, shame, depression, anger, powerlessness or rejection—do you personally identify with the most? Was there any specific event in your life that caused you to feel that way?

We continue to struggle with these mental and emotional issues because we are not living as God designed us to live. We are like cars without gas trying to travel down the road. No matter how good the car looks it cannot fulfill its purpose without gas. Human effort through appearance, performance and social status cannot recapture what Adam and Eve lost.

Consider Solomon, who was king of a nation at its greatest prominence. He had it all: position, power, wealth (so much so that we still hear of King Solomon's mines!), God-given wisdom and more. God gave Solomon more wisdom than any other mortal who has ever lived and with that wisdom came the ability to interpret what he discovered. With all that going for him, Solomon still sought to find purpose and meaning in life apart from God. And what did he conclude when all was said and done? "Vanity of vanities! All is vanity" (Ecclesiastes 1:2). In other words, life lived apart from God is futile.

God had a plan to restore fallen humankind, but first He had to convince us that self-help and human effort cannot meet our needs. He did this by making a covenant with humankind based on the concept of law. If we could live according to the law by human effort, then we would be blessed. If we couldn't, we would be cursed. Naturally we couldn't, so the law became a curse for us because it was powerless to give us life (see Galatians 3:10,21). This was part of the plan, since God intended the law to be a tutor to lead us to Christ (see Galatians 3:24). He had to make us aware of our depravity so that He could bring us back to Him.

THE GOOD NEWS: JESUS CAME TO GIVE US LIFE!

The only possible answer to our human depravity is to restore our relationship with God—to reconnect our spirit with God's Spirit and be alive again spiritually. This is not something we can accomplish ourselves, and this is why God sent Jesus to undo the works of Satan, who had deceived Eve, resulting in the sin that separated her and Adam from God.

Jesus was like the first man—Adam—in that He was both physically and spiritually alive. Unlike Adam, Jesus never sinned. He modeled for us how a spiritually alive person can live in this fallen world so long as that life is lived dependent on the Father. Jesus gave us more than an example, however; He came to give us life. He said, "I came that they may have life, and have it abundantly" (John 10:10).

The Gospel of John records, "In Him was life, and the life was the Light of men" (John 1:4). Notice that light does not produce life. Rather, spiritual life is the light of the world. Jesus said, "I am the resurrection and the life; he who believes in Me will live even if he dies" (John 11:25). Simply put, believers will continue to live *spiritually*, even when they die *physically*.

What Adam lost was *life*—what Jesus came to give us is *life*, which means that our soul is again in union with God. The moment we are born again, our spirit is reconnected to God's Spirit, and His Spirit "testifies with our spirit that we are children of God" (Romans 8:16).

Life, Acceptance, Security and Significance Restored in Christ

Eternal life is not something we get when we die. In 1 John 5:12, the apostle John wrote, "He who has the Son has the life; he who does not have the Son of God does not have the life." The moment we receive Christ, we are given the right to be called children of God (see John 1:12). Having the life of Christ within us is what makes possible the restoration of what Adam and Eve lost in the Fall, and our struggles to establish an identity, to be accepted, secure and significant are now met in Christ.

Have participants read the list on the following page aloud (found in the student guide as well) as a group.

WHO I AM IN CHRIST

I Am Accepted

John 1:12	I am God's child.
John 15:15	I am Christ's friend.
Romans 5:1	I have been justified.
1 Corinthians 6:17	I am united with the Lord, and I am one spirit with Him.
1 Corinthians 6:19-20	I have been bought with a price. I belong to God.
1 Corinthians 12:27	I am a member of Christ's Body.
Ephesians 1:1	I am a saint.
Ephesians 1:5	I have been adopted as God's child.
Ephesians 2:18	I have direct access to God through the Holy Spirit.
Colossians 1:14	I have been redeemed and forgiven of all my sins.
Colossians 2:10	I am complete in Christ.

I Am Secure

Romans 8:1-2	I am free from condemnation.
Romans 8:28	I am assured that all things work together for good.
Romans 8:31-34	I am free from any condemning charges against me.
Romans 8:35-39	I cannot be separated from the love of God.
2 Corinthians 1:21-22	I have been established, anointed and sealed by God.
Philippians 1:6	I am confident that the good work God has begun in me will be perfected.
Philippians 3:20	I am a citizen of heaven.
Colossians 3:3	I am hidden with Christ in God.
2 Timothy 1:7	I have not been given a spirit of fear but of power, love and a sound mind.
Hebrews 4:16	I can find grace and mercy to help in time of need.
1 John 5:18	I am born of God and the evil one cannot touch me.

I Am Significant

Matthew 5:13-14	I am the salt and light of the earth.
John 15:1,5	I am a branch of the true vine, a channel of His life.
John 15:16	I have been chosen and appointed to bear fruit.
Acts 1:8	I am a personal witness of Christ.
1 Corinthians 3:16	I am God's temple.
2 Corinthians 5:17-21	I am a minister of reconciliation for God.
2 Corinthians 6:1	I am God's coworker (see 1 Corinthians 3:9).
Ephesians 2:6	I am seated with Christ in the heavenly realm.
Ephesians 2:10	I am God's workmanship.
Ephesians 3:12	I may approach God with freedom and confidence.
Philippians 4:13	I can do all things through Christ who strengthens me.

Many new believers and those who struggle in their walk with God may find it difficult to believe these verses truly describe them. However, each statement is true because of who we are in Christ. If *God* says it's true, it *is* true, regardless of how we feel or whether or not we fully understand it.

As you lead participants through this course, together you are going to learn more about your identity and position in Christ and how that works out in day-to-day life. What is important right now is to know that as Christians we are accepted by God because of what Christ has already done for us. We are secure in Christ regardless of our circumstances, and we are significant because of who we are in Christ. The beloved Ethel Waters, who first coined the phrase "God don't make no junk," knew this to be an absolute truth. We too will discover our purpose for being here on this earth as we grow in our relationship with Christ.

WITNESS

The following question will help participants begin to formulate ideas for sharing their faith with others. Ask volunteers to offer suggestions for witnessing to nonbelievers, and encourage participants to write down ideas in their student guide.

> How would you explain to a not-yet Christian the truth that ultimately his or her basic needs for life, identity, acceptance and security can be met in Christ?

GROUP DISCUSSION QUESTIONS

Instruct participants to form small groups of four to six, and assign each group several questions to discuss. Allow several minutes for discussion; then bring the whole group back together, and have volunteers from each small group share their group's questions and answers.

1. Consider Adam and Eve's daily life before the Fall. How was their life different from yours?

2. What was the effect of Adam and Eve's sin on our physical bodies?

3. What was the effect of Adam and Eve's sin on our emotions?

When do you recall becoming aware of feelings of guilt, powerlessness and rejection?

Which feelings do you particularly identify with?

4. What did Jesus come to give us?

5. What impact did reading the "Who I Am in Christ" list have on you?

Which verses were especially meaningful and why?

6. If God says something about you that doesn't *feel* true or match your self-perception, how should you respond? Why?

TAKING IT WITH YOU

The following information is included in the student guide and is intended for participants to use during the upcoming week. Direct participants to this section and encourage them to do the quiet-time suggestion and to consider the Big Question before the next session.

SUGGESTION FOR QUIET TIME

Read the "Who I Am in Christ" list out loud every day. Pick one of the truths each day that is particularly relevant to you. Spend some time reading the corresponding Bible verse(s) in context and ask the Lord to help you understand His Word more fully.

THE BIG QUESTION

Before the next session, consider the following question:

> Suppose you are talking to someone who is not yet a Christian. How would you summarize the gospel message in a few sentences?

Note
1. Dov Peretz Elkins, *Glad to Be Me: Building Self-Esteem in Yourself and Others*, rev. ed. (Rochester, NY: Growth Associates, 1989), n.p.

A NEW IDENTITY IN CHRIST

THEREFORE FROM NOW ON WE RECOGNIZE NO ONE ACCORDING TO THE
FLESH; EVEN THOUGH WE HAVE KNOWN CHRIST ACCORDING TO THE FLESH,
YET NOW WE KNOW HIM IN THIS WAY NO LONGER. THEREFORE IF ANYONE
IS IN CHRIST, HE IS A NEW CREATURE; THE OLD THINGS PASSED AWAY;
BEHOLD, NEW THINGS HAVE COME.
2 CORINTHIANS 5:16-17

SESSION OVERVIEW

OBJECTIVE

In this session you will help participants understand what it means to be a new creation in Christ so that they can be firmly rooted in Him and set on the path of sanctification, or conforming to the image of God.

FOCUS TRUTH

The decision to receive new life in Christ by faith is a defining moment that results in becoming a new creation in Christ. As Christians, we have been transferred out of the kingdom of darkness and into the kingdom of God's beloved Son.

BRIEFING

When we accept Jesus as our Savior, He changes our very nature—we are no longer people who are displeasing to God but people in whom He delights. This can be hard for some to accept because they don't *feel* any different or because of what they have believed about themselves in the past. We are assured, however, in God's Word that this happens regardless of what we feel or believe about ourselves.

Going Deeper

You can explore the theological aspects of this topic in more detail by reading God's Power at Work in You and Overcoming Negative Self-Image.[1]

A NEW IDENTITY IN CHRIST

THEREFORE FROM NOW ON WE RECOGNIZE NO ONE ACCORDING TO THE FLESH; EVEN THOUGH WE HAVE KNOWN CHRIST ACCORDING TO THE FLESH, YET NOW WE KNOW HIM IN THIS WAY NO LONGER. THEREFORE IF ANYONE IS IN CHRIST, HE IS A NEW CREATURE; THE OLD THINGS PASSED AWAY; BEHOLD, NEW THINGS HAVE COME.

2 CORINTHIANS 5:16-17

WELCOME

Welcome participants and ask a volunteer to open the meeting in prayer. Give a brief overview of last session's message: Because of the Fall, we are born spiritually dead and in need of salvation—and the only way to salvation is through God's Son, Jesus Christ. Invite volunteers to share their ideas for how to share the gospel message in a few sentences. After a few have shared, make the observation that most people do not inherently feel good about themselves; many question who they are and why they are here on this earth.

Direct participants to page 12 in their student guides and ask them to place a check mark next to the statement in each set that best describes them. (**Note:** Participants can share their answers with the group if they want to, but some may prefer not to.)

❑ I often feel that God has rejected me.

❑ Sometimes I think God accepts me, but there are times when He doesn't.

❑ I believe that God always accepts me.

❑ I don't feel good about myself.

❑ I am just an average person who tries to contribute something to life.

❑ I know who I am and why God created me.

❑ I often doubt whether I will go to heaven when I die.

❑ I hope that I will go to heaven when I die.

❑ I'm certain that I will be with Jesus when I die.

Invite volunteers to share about the events or people that influenced their life (negatively or positively) in ways that prompted them to choose the statements they did. Allow participants to volunteer to share—some may not be comfortable sharing, so it could be awkward if you were to call on them.

WORSHIP

Spend a few minutes worshiping the Lord through prayer, song, praise or testimonies shared by volunteers.

WORD

 The Word section is available on the Beta DVD, or you can present the information yourself in a lecture format.

Share the following illustration:

A circuit preacher was making rounds from one settlement to another on the western frontier of America in the late nineteenth century. A raiding party had left a young Greek immigrant boy orphaned with nobody to care for him. The preacher had no choice but to take him along. Peter turned out to be an incorrigible kid, and it became obvious that the preacher couldn't do his work and provide for him.

The preacher heard about a Christian family named Smith that had recently settled near one of his routes. He asked them if they would prayerfully assume responsibility for the boy and they agreed. The Smith family had a son named Sammy who was about Peter's age, and they became the best of friends, even though Peter continued to be difficult.

Mr. and Mrs. Smith warned the boys not to go near the swamp that was believed to be contaminated. Peter wouldn't listen, and he managed to work his way through the barbed wire fence and go swimming. He must have scratched himself on the rusty fence because he fell deathly ill with an infection and had to be quarantined. Peter's life hung in the balance, and Sammy could only watch and pray as he peered at Peter through an open door. Then one afternoon, Mr. and Mrs. Smith had to make a trip to town to get some supplies. They warned Sammy not to go near Peter; but when they came home, they found the two boys fast asleep in each other's arms. Nobody understands the providence of God, but in this case Peter got well and Sammy got sick. So sick, in fact, that he died.

The circuit preacher had all but forgotten about Peter when several years later he was making his rounds near the Smith home. Recalling the forgotten incident, he decided to make a visit to see what happened to the little orphaned Greek boy. As he approached the farm, he recognized Mr. Smith, but he didn't recognize the young man by his side. "By the way, whatever happened to that incorrigible kid I dropped off a few years back?" he asked Mr. Smith.

Mr. Smith reached up and put his arms around the shoulders of the young man and said, "I want you to meet Peter Smith. We adopted him."

You, too, have been adopted—into the family of God. According to 1 Peter 2:9-10,

But you are a chosen race, a royal priesthood, a holy nation, a people for God's own possession, so that you may proclaim the excellencies of Him who has called you out of darkness into His marvelous light; for you once were not a people, but now you are the people of God; you had not received mercy, but now you have received mercy.

Consider what this young orphaned boy must have thought about himself after the tragedy that left him homeless and destitute. Most likely, he didn't feel much different from how Adam and Eve felt about themselves after the Fall. Many people today struggle with negative self-image. According to Ephesians 2:3, before Christ we were "by nature children of wrath." In other words, we were offensive to God and there was nothing we could do about it! However, when we accept Jesus Christ as our Savior, it is the defining moment of our existence. Everything changes as we pass from spiritual death to life, from the kingdom of darkness to the kingdom of God's dear Son.

A NEW CREATURE

Share what the Bible has to say about how we change when we accept Jesus into our lives.

1. According to the Bible, we were "formerly darkness, but now [we] are Light in the Lord" (Ephesians 5:8).
   Discuss: Can a person be both light and darkness?
2. "For He rescued us from the domain of darkness, and transferred us to the kingdom of His beloved Son" (Colossians 1:13).
   Discuss: Can a person live in both spiritual kingdoms?
3. "If anyone is in Christ, he is a new creature; the old things passed away; behold, new things have come" (2 Corinthians 5:17).
   Discuss: Can you be partly an old creation and partly a new creation?

Consider the following illustration:

In Arizona, city parks and boulevards are decorated with ornamental orange trees that are a much hardier stock than the trees that produce the sweet oranges we eat. Because they can survive colder temperatures, they are used for rootstock.

The ornamental orange is allowed to grow to a certain height; then it is cut off, and a new life (such as a navel orange branch) is grafted into it. Everything that grows above the graft takes on the new nature of the sweet orange. Everything below the graft retains the physical characteristics of the ornamental orange. Only one tree remains when it is fully grown. The *physical* growth of the tree is still dependent on the roots that go deep into the soil for water and nutrition. What grows above the graft takes on the nature of what was grafted onto it.

People don't look at a grove of navel oranges in Arizona and exclaim, "That's not an orange grove; it's just a bunch of rootstock!" Instead, they see the fruit and identify the trees as navel orange trees.

Jesus said, "So then, you will know them by their fruits" (Matthew 7:20). Paul said, "Therefore from now on we recognize no one according to the flesh" (2 Corinthians 5:16). As Christians, we are not recognized by our natural heritage—as descendants of Adam and Eve—but by our spiritual heritage—who we are in Christ. We are new creations; we have become partakers of Jesus Christ's divine nature (see 2 Peter 1:4). It was prophesied in the Old Testament that believers would receive a new heart and a new spirit (see Ezekiel 11:19). The moment we were born again, we inherited a whole new core identity. At the very heart of every believer is a new seed of life that is waiting to take root and sprout in righteousness.

Jesus explained in John 15:1-5 that we have been grafted into Him; He is the vine and we are the branches. He prunes every branch that does not bear fruit. As the branches, we must remain connected to the vine in order to flourish and bear fruit. Spiritual growth in the Christian life requires that we have a relationship with God, the fountain of spiritual life. As in nature, unless there is some seed or root of life within an organism, no growth can take place. A relationship with God brings a new seed or root of life. Paul wrote, "Therefore as you have received Christ Jesus the Lord, so walk in Him, having been firmly rooted and now being built up in Him" (Colossians 2:6-7).

Pause for Thought
As a new creation in Christ, how would you describe yourself? Are you a sinner saved by grace, or are you a saint who sins?

A SAINT, NOT A SINNER

"While we were yet sinners, Christ died for us" (Romans 5:8). This verse implies that once we become Christians, we are no longer identified by God as sinners—we are saved by grace. Paul identified believers as "saints by calling" (1 Corinthians 1:2). So then, if we are no longer sinners in terms of our core identity, what are we?

Unbelievers are identified as sinners over three hundred times in the New Testament. Born-again believers, on the other hand, are identified over two hundred times as holy ones, righteous ones or saints. If you have received Jesus as your Lord, you are not a forgiven sinner but a redeemed saint. The moment you became a Christian, your core identity—who you really are deep down inside—changed. You were no longer excluded from God but accepted, secure and significant in Christ.

One lady commented, "I used to think of myself as a filthy dog with a white coat. I knew that I was covered by the righteousness of Christ, but deep down I still believed that I was an abomination to God. Now I'm starting to realize that I've actually become a clean dog!" Even new Christians are saints because the term "saint" describes a Christian's new identity and position in Christ, not necessarily his or her maturity as a Christian.

ALIVE IN CHRIST

Being called a saint is consistent with our new identity and position in Christ. In the six chapters of the book of Ephesians, the phrases "in Christ," "in the beloved" or "in Him" occur approximately 40 times with regard to believers. These phrases mean that our souls are in union with God and that is what spiritual life really is. Instead of being "objects of wrath," we have become partakers of God's divine nature (see 2 Peter 1:4).

Have participants read the following list aloud (from their student guide) as a group:

IN CHRIST

Since I Am in Christ

Matthew 5:13	I am the salt of the earth.
Matthew 5:14	I am the light of the world.
John 1:12	I am a God's child.
John 15:1, 5	I am a branch of the true vine, a channel of Christ's life.
John 15:15	I am Christ's friend.
John 15:16	I have been chosen and appointed to bear fruit.
Romans 6:18	I am a slave of righteousness.
Romans 6:22	I am enslaved to God.
Romans 8:14-15	I am a son (or daughter) of God.
Romans 8:17	I am a joint heir with Christ, sharing His inheritance with Him.
1 Corinthians 3:16	I am God's temple.
1 Corinthians 6:17	I am united with the Lord, and I am one spirit with Him.
1 Corinthians 12:27	I am a member of Christ's Body.
2 Corinthians 5:17	I am a new creation.
2 Corinthians 5:18-19	I am reconciled to God and am a minister of reconciliation.
Galatians 3:26-28	I am a son (or daughter) of God and one in Christ.
Galatians 4:6-7	I am an heir of God since I am a son (or daughter) of God.
Ephesians 1:1	I am a saint.
Ephesians 2:10	I am God's workmanship.
Ephesians 2:19	I am a fellow citizen with the rest of God's people in His family.
Ephesians 3:1; 4:1	I am a prisoner of Christ.
Ephesians 4:24	I am righteous and holy.
Philippians 3:20	I am a citizen of heaven.
Colossians 3:3	I am hidden with Christ in God.
Colossians 3:4	I am an expression of the life of Christ because He is my life.
Colossians 3:12	I am chosen of God, holy and dearly loved.
1 Thessalonians 1:4	I am chosen and dearly loved by God.
1 Thessalonians 5:5	I am a son (or daughter) of light and not of darkness.
Hebrews 3:1	I am a holy brother (or sister), partaker of a heavenly calling.
Hebrews 3:14	I am a partaker of Christ . . . I share in His life.
1 Peter 2:5	I am one of God's living stones and am being built up as a spiritual house.
1 Peter 2:9	I am a chosen race, a royal priesthood, a holy nation, a people for God's own possession to proclaim the excellencies of Him.
1 Peter 2:11	I am an alien and a stranger to this world in which I temporarily live.
1 Peter 5:8	I am an enemy of the devil.
1 John 3:1-2	I am now a child of God. I will resemble Christ when He returns.
1 John 5:18	I am born of God and the evil one cannot touch me.
Exodus 3:14; John 8:58; 1 Corinthians 15:10	I am not the great I AM, but by the grace of God, I am who I am.

A Whole New Person

If we think of ourselves as forgiven sinners but still sinners, what are we likely to do? Sin, of course! In order to live a truly righteous life, we would have to be new creations in Christ; and God has already accomplished that for us.

"But as many as received Him, to them He gave the right to become children of God, even to those who believe in His name" (John 1:12). In order to appropriate the new life and identity we have been given in Christ, we must believe that we really are children of God. According to the apostle John, knowing who we are as children of God purifies us (see 1 John 3:1-3).

Suppose a woman jailed for prostitution were given the news that the king had issued a decree stating that all prostitutes had been forgiven their past transgressions. Of course, the woman would be very happy, but would the words of the king's decree change how she felt about herself? Perhaps slightly. Would it change her behavior? Probably not.

Now suppose the king's decree stated not only that the woman was forgiven but also that she was to become the king's bride—and the queen? Would that news change how the woman felt about herself? Absolutely! Would it change her behavior? Yes! Her behavior would reflect her newfound status as a role model for the kingdom.

Just as the woman in the illustration, we have been forgiven for our sins by the King of kings and have been made the Bride of Christ!

The Full Gospel

In session 1, we explored the fact that we were all born physically alive but spiritually dead because sin had separated us from God. Suppose you happened upon the body of a man who had recently died from a horrible disease. If you had the power to restore life to the man, it would be a temporary fix unless you also possessed the power to cure the disease that killed him. Paul wrote that our sin is the disease that leads to our death (see Romans 6:23). Jesus went to the cross and died for our sins, but that is not the whole gospel. He also came to give us eternal life. "But the free gift of God is eternal life in Christ Jesus our Lord" (Romans 6:23). Thank God for Good Friday, but the Resurrection is what we celebrate every Easter.

If we knew only half of the truth—that Jesus died to cure the disease that caused us to die—we would believe that we are forgiven sinners. This in itself would not enormously affect our self-perception and how we live. It is only through understanding the whole gospel—that we are alive and free in Christ—that we can change how we live.

Some might say:

- **"You don't know what's been done to me."** It doesn't change who you are in Christ.
- **"You don't know how bad I've been."** It doesn't change who you are in Christ.
- **"You don't know what failures I've had as a Christian."** It doesn't change who you are in Christ. Christ loved you when you were still a sinner. That hasn't stopped now that you're His.
- **"But what about my future sins?"** When Christ died once for all our sins (see Romans 6:10), how many of your sins were yet to be committed?
- **"Wouldn't I be filled with pride if I believed all those things about myself?"** Your new identity in Christ is not something you have earned. It's a free gift made possible by the grace of God alone. You are not saved by how you behave; you are saved by what you believe.

Christ loved us when we were still sinners. That hasn't stopped now that we're His children.

Pleasing to God

Christians are not perfect. We are growing in Christ, so we are likely to sin (and we sin often in our early stages of growth). However, sinning doesn't make us sinners any more than sneezing makes us sneezers. What we do does not determine who we are in Christ; who we are in

Christ determines what we do. That is one big reason why the Holy Spirit is bearing witness with our spirit that we are "children of God" (Romans 8:16). We are not working for our salvation—we are working it out (see Philippians 2:12). We are not trying to become children of God—we are already His children and we are becoming like Christ.

Being a saint means that we have the capacity to choose not to sin. The apostle John wrote, "My little children, I am writing these things to you so that you may not sin" (1 John 2:1). Fortunately, John didn't end there. "And if anyone sins, we have an Advocate with the Father, Jesus Christ the righteous; and He Himself is the propitiation for our sins" (1 John 2:1-2). John also clarified that being a saint does not mean that we are living in a state of sinless perfection: "If we say that we have no sin, we are deceiving ourselves and the truth is not in us" (1 John 1:8). We are saints who sometimes sin.

Some Christians live in constant fear of God's judgment, thinking *If I make one mistake, God's anger is going to fall on me*. Take heart, for God's anger has already fallen. It fell on Christ. We are not sinners in the hands of an angry God; we are saints in the hands of a loving God. He has called us to come into His presence with our hearts washed clean, with confidence and full assurance (see Ephesians 3:12; Hebrews 10:19-22).

Can anything change the fact that we are children of our natural parents? Of course not. We are forever connected to our parents because we share their DNA. There are many things we can do that would affect the harmony of our relationship with them, but we can never change the fact that we are related to our parents by blood.

When we were born again, we became God's children. *Nothing* can separate us from His love (see Romans 8:39). We have His spiritual DNA because His Spirit lives in us (see Romans 8:9). We have become partakers of His divine nature (see 2 Peter 1:4). No one can snatch us out of His hand (see John 10:28). If we are truly born again, we are related to Christ by blood and are joint heirs with Him.

Not Condemned

Just as we can disrupt the harmony of our relationship with our earthly parents, we can also disrupt the harmony of our relationship with our heavenly Father.

What is the appropriate thing to do, when we do something that we know is wrong or displeasing to God and we are ashamed of our actions? We must simply go to God and agree with Him that we were wrong (confess our sin); then we must turn away from our sin, knowing that we are already forgiven because of Christ's sacrifice.

We can always be honest with God, because we are already forgiven. Paul wrote, "Therefore there is now no condemnation for those who are in Christ Jesus" (Romans 8:1). We can't earn our way back into His good grace any more than we could earn it in the first place; each one of us has received it because of what Jesus has done for us. Realizing that truth, we can turn back to God in repentance when we have sinned, knowing that we are already forgiven. Such honest confession is key to becoming mature as Christians.

Pause for Thought
Imagine that you have believed a lie of the enemy and done something that you know is wrong. What is an appropriate thing to do? What can you do if you feel condemned?

DISTINGUISHING CHRISTIANITY FROM FALSE RELIGIONS

Every religion demands performance for acceptance—except Christianity. God's grace is what sets Christianity apart from the rules and rituals of false religions. God loves us, not because we are lovable, but because God is love. It is His nature to love us. If we performed better, He wouldn't love us any more than He does now. We are unconditionally loved and accepted because such love and acceptance is rooted in the nature of God. We can live our lives openly and honestly before Him, knowing that He already knows everything about us—including our thoughts and intentions (see Hebrews 4:12). Therefore, when we sin, we simply admit it openly and honestly with God. Living in the light is based on a true knowledge of God's love and grace.

Many people have found it helpful to speak the following declaration about their heavenly Father:

The Truth About Your Father God

I renounce the lie that my Father God is	I choose to believe the truth that my Father God is
Distant and disinterested	**Intimate and involved** [SEE PSALM 139:1-18]
Insensitive and uncaring	**Kind and compassionate** [SEE PSALM 103:8-14]
Stern and demanding	**Accepting and filled with joy and love** [SEE ZEPHANIAH 3:17; ROMANS 15:7]
Passive and cold	**Warm and affectionate** [SEE ISAIAH 40:11; HOSEA 11:3-4]
Absent or too busy for me	**Always with me and eager to be with me** [SEE JEREMIAH 31:20; EZEKIEL 34:11-16; HEBREWS 13:5]
Impatient, angry and rejecting	**Patient and slow to anger** [SEE EXODUS 34:6; 2 PETER 3:9]
Mean, cruel or abusive	**Loving, gentle and protective** [SEE JEREMIAH 31:3; ISAIAH 42:3; PSALM 18:2]
Trying to take all the fun out of life	**Trustworthy and wants to give me a full life; His will is good, perfect and acceptable for me** [SEE LAMENTATIONS 3:22-23; JOHN 10:10; ROMANS 12:1-2]
Controlling or manipulative	**Full of grace and mercy, and He gives me freedom to fail** [SEE LUKE 15:11-16; HEBREWS 4:15-16]
Condemning or unforgiving	**Tenderhearted and forgiving; His heart and arms are always open to me** [SEE PSALM 130:1-4; LUKE 15:17-24]
A nit-picking, demanding perfectionist	**Committed to my growth and proud of me as His beloved child** [SEE ROMANS 8:28-29; HEBREWS 12:5-11; 2 CORINTHIANS 7:4]

I AM THE APPLE OF HIS EYE!
(See Deuteronomy 32:9-10.)

WITNESS

The following question will help participants begin to formulate ideas for sharing their faith with others. Ask volunteers to offer suggestions for witnessing to nonbelievers, and encourage participants to write down ideas in their student guide.

What Adam and Eve lost in the Fall was life; Jesus came to give us life. People don't like to be judged, and thus calling them sinners may be counterproductive to what you are trying to accomplish. Pascal said there is a God-shaped vacuum in every person. People *need* new life in Christ. How might knowing that help you in witnessing to others?

GROUP DISCUSSION QUESTIONS

Instruct participants to form small groups of four to six, and assign each group several questions to discuss. Allow several minutes for discussion; then bring the whole group back together, and have volunteers from each small group share their group's questions and answers.

1. To what degree have you struggled with a negative self-image?

   What caused you to feel that way about yourself?

2. Have you understood yourself to be a sinner or a saint? What or who contributed to that assessment?

3. Why is it so important to understand the whole gospel?

4. What should we do when we sin?

5. What has been your perception of God in the past and what contributed to it?

   What is your perception now? Why?

TAKING IT WITH YOU

The following information is included in the student guide and is intended for participants to use during the upcoming week. Direct participants to this section and encourage them to do the quiet-time suggestion and to consider the Big Question before your next session.

SUGGESTION FOR QUIET TIME

Read the entire "In Christ" list out loud every day this week. Look up each verse in the list in your Bible and read it. Then do the same for the verses that reveal the truth about God.

THE BIG QUESTION

Before the next session, consider the following question:

How does a Christian walk by faith?

Note
1. Neil T. Anderson and Robert L. Saucy, *God's Power at Work in You* (Eugene, OR: Harvest House, 2001); Neil T. Anderson and Dave Park, *Overcoming Negative Self-Image* (Ventura, CA: Regal Books, 2003).

LIVING BY FAITH

WITHOUT FAITH IT IS IMPOSSIBLE TO PLEASE HIM, FOR
HE WHO COMES TO GOD MUST BELIEVE THAT HE IS AND
THAT HE IS A REWARDER OF THOSE WHO SEEK HIM.
HEBREWS 11:6

SESSION OVERVIEW

OBJECTIVE

In this session, you will help participants understand the nature of faith and how Christians can live by faith in the power of the Holy Spirit.

FOCUS TRUTH

Relativism is the predominant philosophy in our post-modern world. In contrast, Christianity asserts that God is the ultimate reality and that His Word is absolute truth. Creation cannot determine what is true and what is real; only the creator can do that. Truth is something we choose to believe or not, and choosing to believe what God says is true is the only means by which we can live a righteous life.

BRIEFING

It may surprise some people to realize that everybody lives by faith and that Christian faith means simply making a choice to believe that what God says is true. It is important as Christians that we make a definite commitment to believe what God says is true no matter what our feelings tell us.

LIVING BY FAITH

WITHOUT FAITH IT IS IMPOSSIBLE TO PLEASE HIM, FOR
HE WHO COMES TO GOD MUST BELIEVE THAT HE IS AND
THAT HE IS A REWARDER OF THOSE WHO SEEK HIM.
HEBREWS 11:6

WELCOME

Welcome participants and open the meeting in prayer, asking God for guidance as you teach His truth during this session.

Direct participants to the following statements on page 18 in their student guide. Give them two to three minutes to complete the statements; then invite volunteers to share what they've written.

- Faith is . . .
- I would have more faith if I . . .
- The difference between Christian faith and the faith of other religions is . . .
- I live by faith when I . . .

After several have shared their statements, read the following excerpt from *The Sacred Diary of Adrian Plass*:

Monday January 6
Bought a really good book about faith. It's called "Goodness Gracious—In God's Name, What on Earth Are We Doing for Heaven's Sake?" A very witty title I feel.

It's all about how Christians should be able to move mountains by faith, if they are really tuned to God. Very inspiring.

Waited till there was no one around, then practiced with a paper clip. Put it on my desk and stared at it, willing it to move. Nothing! Tried commanding it in a loud voice.

Tuesday January 7
Had another go with the paper clip tonight. Really took authority over it. Couldn't get it to budge.

Told God I'd give up anything He wanted if He would just make it move half an inch. Nothing!

All rather worrying really. If you only need faith the size of a mustard seed to move a mountain, what hope is there for me when I can't even get a paper clip to do what it's told!

Saturday January 11
Got up early today to have a last go at that blasted paper clip. Ended up hissing viciously at it, trying not to wake everybody up. When I gave up and opened the door, I found Anne and Gerald listening outside in their night clothes, looking quite anxious.

Anne said, "Darling, why did you tell that paper clip you'd straighten it out if it didn't soon get its act together?"[1]

WORSHIP

Spend a few minutes worshiping the Lord through prayer, song, praise or testimonies shared by volunteers.

WORD

 The Word section is available on the Beta DVD, or you can present the information yourself in a lecture format.

Share the following quote about victorious Christian living from Hudson Taylor, an Englishman often credited for bringing the gospel to China:

I felt the ingratitude, the danger, the sin of not living nearer to God. I prayed, agonized, fasted, strove, made resolutions, read the Word more diligently, sought more time for meditation—but without avail. Every day, almost every hour, the consciousness of sin oppressed me.

I knew that if only I could abide in Christ all would be well, but I could not . . . . each day brought its register of sin and failure, of lack of power. To will was indeed present within me, but how to perform I found not. . . . Then came the question, is there no rescue? Must it be thus to the end—constant conflict, and too often defeat? I hated myself, my sin, yet gained no strength against it. . . . I felt I was a child of God . . . but to rise to my privileges as a child, I was utterly powerless.

All the time I felt assured that there was in Christ all I needed, but the practical question was—how to get it out. . . . I strove for faith, but it would not come: I tried to exercise it, but in vain. . . . I prayed for faith, but it came not. What was I to do?

When my agony of soul was at its height, a sentence in a letter from dear McCarthy was used to remove the scales from my eyes, and the Spirit of God revealed to me the truth of our oneness with Jesus as I had never known it before. (I quote from memory): "But how to get faith strengthened? Not by striving after faith, but by resting on the faithful One."

As I read, I saw it all! "If we believe not, He abideth faithful." I looked to Jesus and saw (and when I saw, oh, how the joy flowed!) that He had said, "I will never leave thee." I thought, "I have striven in vain to rest in Him. I'll strive no more."

I am no better than before. In a sense I do not wish to be. But I am dead, buried with Christ—aye, and risen too! And now Christ lives in me and "the life that I now live in the flesh, I live by faith in the Son of God, who loved me and gave himself up for me." Do not let us consider Him as far off, when God has made us one with Him, members of His body. Nor should we look upon this experience, these truths, as for a few. They are the birthright of every child of God . . . the only power for deliverance from sin or for true service.[2]

Ask a volunteer to read this week's memory verse from Hebrews 11:6: "Without faith it is impossible to please Him, for he who comes to God must believe that He is and that He is a rewarder of those who seek Him." The big question is, What is faith and how do we live by it?

THE ESSENCE OF FAITH

Share the following illustration:

> A mother asked her little boy what he had learned in Sunday School that day. "My teacher told us about Moses, who was being chased by the Egyptians," he replied. "When he came to this big sea, he built a pontoon bridge and hurried all his people across, and when the Egyptians came, he blew up the bridge and they all drowned!"
>
> "Is that what your teacher taught you?" asked his mother.
>
> "No," explained the little boy, "but you wouldn't believe what my teacher really said."

If you've ever asked a child a question, there is no doubt this little boy's answer to his mother does not surprise you. Like many people, the little boy thought that faith was believing in something that isn't true, or that faith is just wishful thinking.

In the New Testament, the English words "faith," "belief" and "trust" are all the same word in the original Greek language. Believing in something means more than giving mental assent or intellectual acknowledgment. Faith is a demonstrated reliance on somebody or something. Consider how important the concept of faith is: We are saved by faith (see Ephesians 2:8-9), and we "walk by faith, not by sight" (2 Corinthians 5:7). In other words, faith is the basis for our salvation and the means by which we live. If we are going to live free in Christ, there are three operating principles of faith that we need to keep in mind.

Faith Depends on Its Object

Everyone lives by faith; the critical issue is *what* we believe or *who* we believe in. Simply telling others to live by faith is meaningless if they have no understanding of the object of their faith. No one can have faith in faith. Faith is dependent on its object.

Some of our faith objects are valid; others are not. For example, think about the last time you were driving a car. No doubt you went through at least one intersection where you had a green light, and without thinking about it, you drove through the intersection. Why? First, you had faith that the light for traffic coming the other direction was red. Second, you believed that the drivers coming from the cross street would stop and obey the signal. That's a lot of faith in a mechanical device and humankind, isn't it? If you didn't have faith in the mechanical stability of the lights at an intersection, you would proceed very cautiously each time you came upon one. Experience has taught you, however, that you can rely on the signal lights at an intersection without thinking much about it. We trust people or things that have proven to be reliable over a long period of time.

The most accepted faith object for humankind is the fixed order of the universe, primarily the solar system. We set our watches, plan our calendars and schedule our days believing that Earth will continue to revolve on its axis and rotate around the sun at its current speed. If Earth's orbit shifted just a few degrees and the sun showed up two hours late, the whole world would be thrown into chaos. The laws governing the physical universe have been among the most trustworthy faith objects we have.

The ultimate faith object, of course, is not the sun but the Son, because "Jesus Christ is the same yesterday and today and forever" (Hebrews 13:8). The fact that God is immutable is what makes Him eminently trustworthy (see Numbers 23:19-20; Malachi 3:6). God cannot change nor can His Word change. "The grass withers, the flower fades, but the word of our God stands forever" (Isaiah 40:8). This eternal consistency is why we can put our complete trust in Him.

Pause for Thought
Have you ever lost faith in someone or something? Were you able to regain your faith? Has this ever happened with your faith in God?

The Measure of Faith Depends on Our Knowledge of the Faith Object

When people struggle with their faith in God, it's not because He has failed or is insufficient—it is because they don't have a true knowledge of who He is. Instead of seeking to know Him, people become disillusioned when God does not respond in the way they expect Him to respond.

If you want your faith in God to increase, you must consciously increase your knowledge of Him. Faith cannot be pumped up by coaching yourself to think, *If only I can believe!* Any attempt to step out on faith beyond that which you know to be true about God and His ways is presumptuous, and the only way to increase your faith is to increase your knowledge of God and His Word, the only legitimate and authoritative faith object. That is why Paul wrote, "So faith comes from hearing, and hearing by the word of Christ" (Romans 10:17).

Pause for Thought
Discuss the practical, tangible potential for your faith to grow as you endeavor to know God through reading and studying the Bible, memorizing Scripture, and spending time with God in prayer and meditation.

Christian faith is only bound by the infinite nature of God! The heroes in Hebrews chapter 11 had great faith, because they had a great God and they knew it. We have a covenant relationship with God that we can count on being true, and He will always keep His Word. It is important to know, however, that God is under no obligation to humankind. We can't maneuver or manipulate Him. God is under obligation to Himself to remain faithful to His covenant promises and His Word. If God declares something to be true, we must simply believe Him and live by faith according to what is true. If God didn't say it, no amount of faith will make it so. Believing doesn't make God's Word true—His Word is true, therefore we believe it.

To illustrate how faith grows, consider the following illustration:

A father stood his young son on a table and encouraged the boy to jump into his arms. The boy hesitated for a moment, unsure whether his father would catch him. Then he leaped off the table into the safety of his father's arms. The father stood the boy back up on the table and then backed further away than the last time. The boy, whose faith had grown, trusted his father to catch him again and jumped. Next, the father took the boy outside and helped him climb onto the branch of a tree. Again, the boy had faith in his father and jumped.

As this boy continues to climb the tree of life, can any human father be the perfect object of his child's faith? No! Eventually, his father will fail him—not because his father wants to, but because his father is only human. When we were children, there was a time when we thought our parents could answer any question and defeat any foe. As we grew up, we realized that our parents make mistakes and aren't perfect. Only God is absolutely perfect and will never fail us.

We have an obligation as parents to do more than lead our children to a saving knowledge of our Lord Jesus Christ. We need to help them understand their spiritual identity and heritage. The object of their faith changes when they become children of God. We can't always be with our children, but their heavenly Father is.

Faith Is an Action Word

When the father was encouraging his son to take a step of faith, did the child believe his father would catch him? Yes. He demonstrated his belief when he jumped. Now, suppose the young boy refused to jump. Suppose the father asked, "Do you believe I will catch you?" If the boy's answer was yes but then he never jumped, did he really believe? Not according to James. Such professions of faith are just wishful thinking.

James wrote, "Even so faith, if it has no works, is dead, being by itself. But someone may well say, 'You have faith and I have works; show me your faith without the works, and I will show you my faith by my works'" (James 2:17-18). In other words, if we really believe, it will affect our walk and our talk—we will live according to what we believe, not what we profess to believe.

DISTORTIONS OF FAITH
New Age and Eastern Religious Philosophies

Faith without action is one distortion, but New Age and Eastern philosophies offer another distortion of what it means to believe. New Age practitioners say, "If you believe hard enough, what you believe will become true." Christianity says, "It is true; therefore, we believe it." Believing something doesn't make it true and not believing something doesn't make it false. For instance, not believing in hell doesn't lower the temperature down there one degree!

Consider the words of Jesus: "For truly I say to you, if you have faith the size of a mustard seed, you will say

to this mountain, 'Move from here to there,' and it will move; and nothing will be impossible to you" (Matthew 17:20). It is correct to point out that the mountain doesn't move until you tell it to move. Faith doesn't work until it is acted upon, which is the point of this passage. It is incorrect to assume that we can believe whatever we want and objects will move simply because we command them to move. Such reasoning is in league with New Age philosophers who teach that we can create reality with our minds. To do that, a person would have to be a god and that is exactly what these New Age believers are teaching.

There is only one creator and only One who can speak into existence something out of nothing. With God all things are possible, and we can do all things (i.e., all things that are consistent with His will and His Word) through Christ who strengthens us (see Philippians 4:13); but we have never been given the privilege to determine for ourselves what is true and decide for ourselves what is God's will. Think about the man who wanted to move the paper clip with his mind. Telekinesis is an occult practice that tries to move matter by mental energy. Now, if God told us to pray that an obstacle should be moved and we prayed by faith in Him, the object would indeed be moved. The difference is that it would not be us who moved it but God.

Distortions such as those we've just discussed often arise when the Church is not living up to its potential. In such times, people think the Church is an infirmary where sick people go. They limp along in unbelief, hoping the Lord will come soon and take them out of their miserable existence. The Church is not an infirmary; it's a military outpost under orders to storm the fortresses of unbelief. Every believer is on active duty, called to take part in fulfilling the Great Commission (see Matthew 28:19-20). Thankfully, the Church has an infirmary that ministers to the weak and the wounded, but the infirmary exists for the purpose of the military outpost. Our real calling is to be change agents in the world, taking a stand, living by faith according to what God says is true and fulfilling our purpose for being here.

Pause for Thought
What distortions of faith have you witnessed in your experience?

The Power of Positive Thinking Versus the Power of Truth Believing

Motivational speakers understand the problem with unbelief. Henry Ford once said, "Whether you think you can or whether you think you can't, you are right."[3] Such optimists stress the power of positive thinking. The following poem further illustrates this point:

> If you think you are beaten—you are.
> If you think you dare not—you don't.
> If you think you'll lose—you've lost.
> For out of the world we find
> That success begins with a fellow's will;
> It's all in the state of mind.
> Life's battles don't always go
> To the stronger or the faster man;
> But sooner or later the man that wins
> Is the one who thinks he can.[4]

We are not called to simply think positive thoughts; we are called to believe the truth. Without God as the object of our faith, thinking is merely a function of the mind—a function that cannot exceed its input and attributes. Attempting to push the mind beyond its limitations will only result in moving from the world of reality to fantasy.

The power of positive thinking is vastly inferior to the power of truth believing. Belief incorporates the mind, but the object of our faith is not limited by it. Faith actually transcends the limitations of the mind and incorporates the real but unseen world. Our faith is as valid as its object, which is the living Christ and written Word of God, the Bible. With the infinite God of the universe as the object of our Christian faith, we can go wherever He leads us and be all that He created us to be.

Someone once said that success comes in *cans* and failure in *cannots*. Believing that we can live a victorious Christian life takes no more effort than believing we cannot. We are called to believe that we *can* walk by faith in the power of the Holy Spirit, that we *can* resist the temptations of the world, the flesh and the devil and that we *can* grow as Christians. It is a choice each of us must make if we desire to grow in Christ.

Ask several volunteers to take turns reading the "Twenty Cans of Success" from their student guides (pp. 20-21). Explain that in reading these truths, participants will build their faith by expanding their knowledge of our faith object—the almighty God. Internalizing these truths from His Word will lift participants from the miry clay of the cannots to say, "I can do all things through Christ who strengthens me" (Philippians 4:13).

TWENTY CANS OF SUCCESS

1. Why should I say I can't when the Bible says I can do all things through Christ who gives me strength? (See Philippians 4:13.)

2. Why should I worry about my needs when I know that God will take care of all my needs according to His riches in glory in Christ Jesus? (See Philippians 4:19.)

3. Why should I fear when the Bible says God has not given me a spirit of fear, but of power, love and a sound mind? (See 2 Timothy 1:7.)

4. Why should I lack faith to live for Christ when God has given me a measure of faith? (See Romans 12:3.)

5. Why should I be weak when the Bible says that the Lord is the strength of my life and that I will display strength and take action because I know God? (See Psalm 27:1; Daniel 11:32.)

6. Why should I allow Satan control over my life when He that is in me is greater than he that is in the world? (See 1 John 4:4.)

7. Why should I accept defeat when the Bible says that God always leads me in victory? (See 2 Corinthians 2:14.)

8. Why should I lack wisdom when I know that Christ became wisdom to me from God and that God gives wisdom to me generously when I ask Him for it? (See 1 Corinthians 1:30; James 1:5.)

9. Why should I be depressed when I can recall to mind God's loving-kindness, compassion, faithfulness and have hope? (See Lamentations 3:21-23.)

10. Why should I worry and be upset when I can cast all my anxieties on Christ who cares for me? (See 1 Peter 5:7.)

11. Why should I ever be in bondage knowing that there is freedom where the Spirit of the Lord is? (See 2 Corinthians 3:17; Galatians 5:1.)

12. Why should I feel condemned when the Bible says there is no condemnation for those who are in Christ Jesus? (See Romans 8:1.)

13. Why should I feel alone when Jesus said He is with me always and He will never leave me nor forsake me? (See Matthew 28:20; Hebrews 13:5.)

14. Why should I feel like I'm cursed or have bad luck when the Bible says that Christ rescued me from the curse of the law that I might receive His Spirit by faith? (See Galatians 3:13-14.)

15. Why should I be unhappy when I, like Paul, can learn to be content whatever the circumstances? (See Philippians 4:11.)

16. Why should I feel worthless when Christ became sin for me so that I might become the righteousness of God? (See 2 Corinthians 5:21.)

17. Why should I feel helpless in the presence of others when I know that if God is for me, who can be against me? (See Romans 8:31.)

18. Why should I be confused when God is the author of peace and He gives me knowledge through His Spirit who lives in me? (See 1 Corinthians 2:12; 14:33.)

19. Why should I feel like a failure when I am more than a conqueror through Christ who loved me? (See Romans 8:37.)

20. Why should I let the pressures of life bother me when I can take courage knowing that Jesus has overcome the world and its problems? (See John 16:33.)

Pause for Thought

Elijah said, "How long will you hesitate between two opinions? If the Lord is God follow him; but if Baal, follow him" (1 Kings 18:21). Will you take this opportunity to make a new commitment to base your life solely on what God says is true, regardless of your feelings or the opinions of others? Spend some time in prayer with the group and tell God what you are going to do.

WITNESS

The following questions will help participants begin to formulate ideas for sharing their faith with others. Ask volunteers to offer suggestions for witnessing to nonbelievers, and encourage participants to write down ideas in their student guide.

1. Think of someone you know who is not yet a Christian. What does the Bible say about why he or she does not yet believe (see Romans 10:14-15; 2 Corinthians 4:4)?

2. How can you share your faith with this person?

3. How can you pray against Satan's blinding?

GROUP DISCUSSION QUESTIONS

Instruct participants to form small groups of four to six, and assign each group several questions to discuss. Allow several minutes for discussion; then bring the whole group back together, and have volunteers from each small group share their group's questions and answers.

1. Have you ever experienced a time when you had to take God at His Word? What happened?

2. Do you agree that everyone lives by faith? Explain your answer.

   How much faith do you think it takes to believe that the whole universe came about by chance?

3. Do you agree that who or what you put your faith in determines whether your faith is effective? Or does it have more to do with how much faith you have?

4. Do you think that we can choose to have faith? Why or why not?

5. Can you think of a time when you asked God to do something and were disappointed because He didn't answer your prayer in the way you wanted? (For example, have you ever prayed faithfully for someone to be healed, but then the person died?) What do you conclude from such difficult experiences?

6. Elijah said, "How long will you hesitate between two opinions? If the LORD is God, follow him; but if Baal, follow him" (1 Kings 18:21). What is keeping you from making a commitment to base your life solely on what God says is true, regardless of your feelings or the opinions of others?

TAKING IT WITH YOU

The following information is included in the student guide and is intended for participants to use during the upcoming week. Direct participants to this section and encourage them to do the quiet-time suggestion and to consider the Big Question before your next session.

SUGGESTION FOR QUIET TIME

Read the "Twenty Cans of Success" list out loud every day. Pick one of the truths that is particularly appropriate to you and make a decision to believe it, regardless of your feelings and circumstances. Commit yourself to step out in faith based on the truth you have learned this week!

THE BIG QUESTION

Before the next session, consider the following question:

How is your perspective of this world different
from that of others and how is it different from
the way God sees the world?

Notes

1. Adrian Plass, *The Sacred Diary of Adrian Plass (Aged 37 ³/₄)* (Grand Rapids, MI: Zondervan Publishing House, 1990), n.p.
2. Dr. and Mrs. Howard Taylor, *Hudson Taylor's Spiritual Secret* (Chicago: Moody Press, 1990), pp. 158-164.
3. Henry Ford, quoted in "Ability Quotes," *Motivational Depot*. http://www.motivational-depot.com/quotes/ability/ability-quotes-h.htm (accessed September 24, 2003).
4. Source unknown.

RESHAPING OUR WORLDVIEW

THEREFORE AS YOU HAVE RECEIVED CHRIST JESUS THE LORD, SO WALK IN HIM,
HAVING BEEN FIRMLY ROOTED AND NOW BEING BUILT UP IN HIM AND ESTABLISHED
IN YOUR FAITH, JUST AS YOU WERE INSTRUCTED, AND OVERFLOWING WITH GRATI-
TUDE. SEE TO IT THAT NO ONE TAKES YOU CAPTIVE THROUGH PHILOSOPHY AND
EMPTY DECEPTION, ACCORDING TO THE TRADITION OF MEN, ACCORDING TO THE
ELEMENTARY PRINCIPLES OF THE WORLD, RATHER THAN ACCORDING TO CHRIST.
COLOSSIANS 2:6-8

SESSION OVERVIEW

OBJECTIVE

In this session, you will help participants understand how worldview affects the way people live. You will also guide them toward adopting a biblical worldview and choosing to believe that what God says is true.

FOCUS TRUTH

The world in which we were raised has influenced our perception of reality. Consequently, we have a tendency to interpret life from a limited worldly perspective. Our worldview is a grid by which we evaluate life experiences. Wisdom is seeing life from God's perspective and evaluating life through the grid of Scripture. To change our worldview requires repentance, which literally means a change of mind.

BRIEFING

It's very easy for people to accept the worldview of their parents, teachers and significant others. As Christians, we must consider our personal worldview and contrast it with God's perspective. Many of us have grown up with beliefs that are not consistent with Scripture. We must grow out of our old ways of thinking and living in order to experience freedom in Christ.

RESHAPING OUR WORLDVIEW

THEREFORE AS YOU HAVE RECEIVED CHRIST JESUS THE LORD, SO WALK IN HIM, HAVING BEEN FIRMLY ROOTED AND NOW BEING BUILT UP IN HIM AND ESTABLISHED IN YOUR FAITH, JUST AS YOU WERE INSTRUCTED, AND OVERFLOWING WITH GRATITUDE. SEE TO IT THAT NO ONE TAKES YOU CAPTIVE THROUGH PHILOSOPHY AND EMPTY DECEPTION, ACCORDING TO THE TRADITION OF MEN, ACCORDING TO THE ELEMENTARY PRINCIPLES OF THE WORLD, RATHER THAN ACCORDING TO CHRIST.

COLOSSIANS 2:6-8

WELCOME

Welcome participants and ask a volunteer to open the meeting in prayer. Review what they learned in the last session and invite volunteers to share their answers to the Big Question. Allow time for a few to share; then introduce this week's message by asking if anyone has heard someone being described as "seeing the world through rose-colored glasses." The implication of this statement is that someone has an overly optimistic view of reality, or that he or she is not seeing life as others do. When someone else's views on reality differ from ours, there will be a disconnection when we try to communicate with that person. In today's session, we are going to take a look at how we perceive reality.

Consider how different your worldview would be if you were raised in a poor rural area in India with no television or radio and no education beyond the sixth grade. Imagine too that you were taught to believe that God is just a higher state of consciousness. What would it be like to live that way and how would it be different from the world in which you currently live?

No doubt if you have a computer with e-mail capability, you've received forwarded quips and quotes. Share the following e-mail that I received regarding bantering between a lawyer and a doctor from a supposedly real court case. It's a great example of communication (or the lack thereof!) between two people who have different views of reality.

Q. Doctor, before you performed the autopsy, did you check for a pulse?
A. No.
Q. Did you check for blood pressure?
A. No.
Q. Did you check for breathing?
A. No.

Q. So, then it is possible that the patient was alive when you began the autopsy?
A. No.
Q. How can you be so sure, Doctor?
A. Because his brain was sitting on my desk in a jar.
Q. But could the patient have still been alive nevertheless?
A. Yes, it is possible that he could have been alive and practicing law.

WORSHIP

Spend a few minutes worshiping the Lord through prayer, song, praise or testimonies shared by volunteers.

WORD

 The Word section is available on the Beta DVD, or you can present the information yourself in a lecture format.

DEFINING THE TERM "WORLDVIEW"

Do you see the world through rose-colored glasses, looking for opportunity in every risk? Or do you look at reality in an overly pessimistic way, seeing the risk in every opportunity? No one is born with a well-defined worldview, and we have all learned to look at the world from a personal perspective. Our present understanding of this world was assimilated from the environment in which we were raised and developed through numerous learning experiences, most of which were informal. It has been said that attitudes are more caught than taught.

There is no society in which all people hold exactly the same worldview. In North America it is politically correct to have tolerance for different opinions and beliefs. The question is, How does our worldview differ from a biblical worldview? To start with, let's put on a different pair of glasses that will allow us to see in broad strokes how people interpret this world from different perspectives.

DIFFERENT WORLDVIEWS

Animism

Animism is the oldest and probably most widely held worldview. It is not considered a world religion because it has never been formalized like Christianity, Islam or Hinduism. It is found in its purest form in preliterate tribal societies, but some elements are found in most modern societies. Animism varies from tribe to tribe and deals with the practical realities of daily life. There are,

however, some general beliefs that are associated with this worldview.

Most animists believe in a creator, or god (or gods), of some kind but see their god or gods as being so far removed from them that it would be hard, if not impossible, to make any connection. The animist is more concerned with a neutral spiritual power (called "mana" in anthropological literature) that is thought to permeate everything in the universe—animal, vegetable and mineral—and with spirits of many types (see figure 4-A).

Mana is thought to be a power much like electricity. Consider how most people use electricity. We turn switches on and off, change light bulbs and plug in extension cords, but that's about the extent of our dealing with electrical currents. When we need to have new wiring installed, we hire electricians—electrical experts. We know that if not handled properly, electricity can be harmful. Animists use spiritual experts to handle problems in the spiritual realm. These experts are usually

Figure 4-A

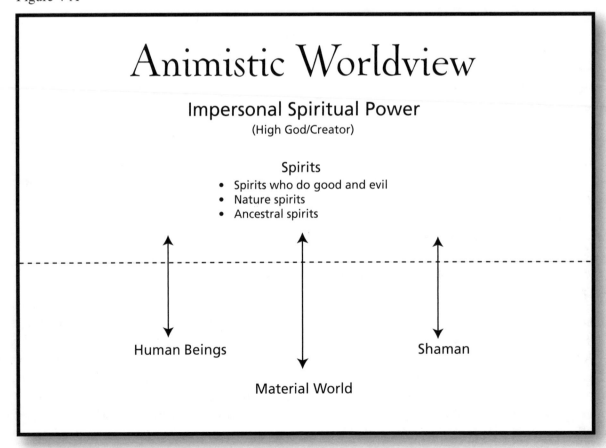

called shamans, witch doctors or medicine men and deal with this impersonal spiritual power because they have special formulas, activities and incantations that they believe manipulate the spirit world.

Animists also believe that if they know the right things to do and the right words to say, they can control or influence spirit beings. These spirit beings are often associated with natural objects or with people who have died, may be good or evil, and have individual identities. This control over spirits is not complete, however, and animists live in constant fear that they might somehow displease the spirit beings and invite retribution. They also fear that an enemy may develop a superior occult skill to direct the power of mana or various other spirits against them.

Animism is found in all parts of the world, even among those who profess to believe one of the world religions. In Thailand, where Buddhism is the dominant religion, a university professor said that he did not know a single intellectual who was not also an animist; the president of the university at which he taught regularly consulted the spirits before making major decisions. In France, there are more magical healers—people who call on this impersonal spiritual power to help in the healing process—than there are medical doctors.

Eastern Religions, or Philosophies

In Eastern religions, there is no personal God. Instead, there is an impersonal cosmic force that permeates everything.

Hinduism is one of the earliest formalized religions, dating back to 1500 B.C. There is, however, not one clear development of thought over the course of its history. Hindu leaders have repeatedly added new concepts—regardless of their compatibility with prior convention—to their belief system. As a result, their religious beliefs have many illogical inconsistencies; however, these inconsistencies are considered unimportant—if considered at all—and do nothing to change their beliefs.

Hinduism became popular in the West when the Maharishi Mahesh Yogi introduced transcendental meditation. His view was that the mind is a snake that you have to neutralize or get out of the way in order to perceive truth directly. This teaching is in stark contrast to Christianity, which teaches against any passivity of the mind, and that the Christian is transformed by the renewing of the mind. Deepak Chopra, M.D., is well known for having introduced Hindu beliefs into mainstream medical education in the West. New Age practitioners adore him because his philosophy is wholistic, but it is totally incompatible with Christianity.

Ayurveda (pronounced ay-yoor-va-duh) is a type of Hinduism that believes that the basis of life is rooted in the nonmaterial world—in a field of energy known as *prana*. According to Ayurveda, all matter (including humans) have at their core a nonmaterial waveform, which is derived from this underlying energy field of pure intelligence. The goal is for each individual to develop the highest level of consciousness and, thereby, attain union with universal intelligence. This is referred to as *moksa* in Hinduism. In moksa, the highest aim is liberation from the cycle of birth, suffering and rebirth (reincarnation). This is principally accomplished by means of higher and higher meditative states until one achieves union with the divine, or ultimate, consciousness. In Hinduism, Karma predetermines a person's birth, place in society, health and length of life on the basis of how well he or she has performed in a previous life.

Taoism (also known as Daosim) is another Eastern philosophy that has filtred into our Western world primarily through medicine. Traditional Chinese medicine is being introduced in the West through acupuncture, acupressure, reflexology, Chinese herbs, etc. Tao has two faces, yin and yang, which oppose each other yet are one. Human beings are said to be inseparable from yin, yang and the world about them. According to this worldview, there is no absolute good or evil, just balance or imbalance, harmony or disharmony.

Such beliefs dramatically affect our worldview and how we live. There is no one way to diagram what they believe since an undefined impersonal energy source permeates everything. There is no creator God, and no need for salvation. You only have to realize that you are god or a god or part of god, and then get in touch with a higher level of consciousness.

MODERN WESTERN WORLDVIEW

The early settlers of America came for the purpose of personal and religious freedom. Our Founding Fathers incorporated the value of the early settlers into our Constitution, setting the standard for a culture with a Judeo-Christian ethic. However, the American culture has changed significantly in the last 50 years.

Rationalism and Naturalism

Rationalism and naturalism have dominated the Western culture throughout most of the twentieth century. Although most people say they believe in God, the majority do not believe that the existence of God significantly impacts their daily life.

According to the modern Western worldview, the world is generally divided into two functional realms: the supernatural realm and the natural realm, as shown in figure 2. All spirit beings, including God, angels and demons, are placed in the supernatural realm because they don't functionally fit with the natural world of scientific rationalism. From this perspective, there is a chasm between the spiritual realm and the natural realm.

Consequently, spiritual principles are considered unnecessary for understanding life; they are, therefore, not an essential part of education. Religion can be left out of our children's science and humanities lessons—it is believed—since the natural realm is thought to be governed by natural laws. God may have created the world and established natural laws that govern the universe, but He is now seated far away on His throne in heaven and doesn't tend to interfere with life on Earth.

As a result, the average person doesn't spend very much time thinking about the purpose and meaning of life. For all practical purposes the world came about by chance; and God, if He exists at all, is irrelevant to daily life.

Postmodernism

The modern Western worldview is in decline now. The emerging worldview is called postmodernism. Most inhabitants of the West have been influenced by both the modern and the postmodern worldviews—the younger you are, the more likely you are to have been influenced by postmodernism. Friedrich Nietzsche summed up postmodernism when he said, "There are many kinds of eyes. . . . Consequently there are many kinds of 'truths,' and consequently there is no truth."[1] Is that true?

While modern Western rationalists and naturalists may not see God as truth, they do not deny the existence of truth itself—truth is something that can be discovered

Figure 4-B

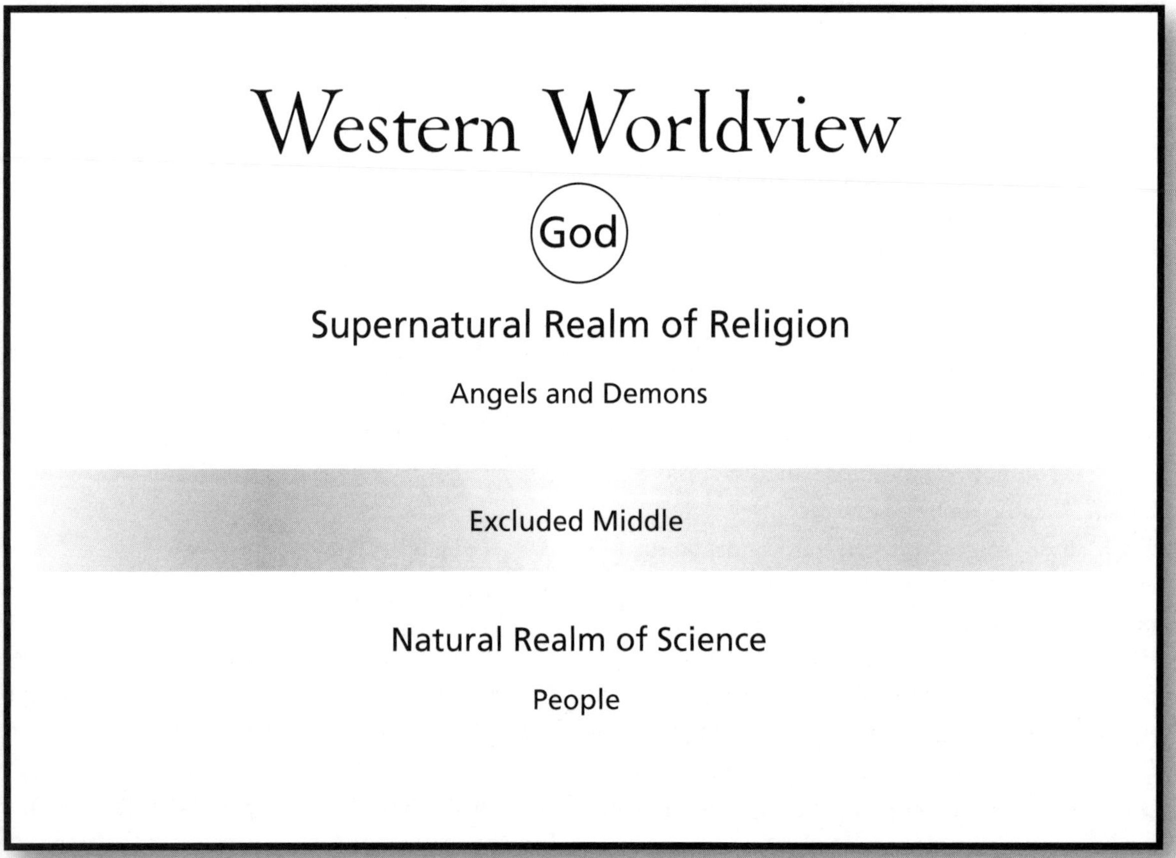

Western Worldview

(God)

Supernatural Realm of Religion

Angels and Demons

Excluded Middle

Natural Realm of Science

People

by empirical research through the scientific method of investigation. However, according to postmodernism there is no absolute truth—at least not as something that stands on its own. Instead, each person determines his or her own version of the truth and standard of morality. For example, university professors report that students increasingly are not willing to say that the Holocaust was wrong. They may admit that it would be wrong for them, but they do not want to impose their values on a different people in a different time.

Postmodernism teaches that truth is determined by humans, and all humans have equally valid perspectives; therefore, everyone's perception of truth is equally valid. Any worldview that claims to be divinely inspired and correct is considered suspect.

Postmodernism doesn't differentiate between what a person thinks or does and the person himself: *Who I am is equal to what I do. If you say that my behavior is wrong, you're judging me. If you disagree with my beliefs, you're disparaging me.* Consequently, there is enormous pressure to accept everybody's lifestyle as true and valid, no matter what it is.

In postmodern society, the Church is under increasing pressure to compromise God-given moral absolutes. It is politically incorrect to say to someone practicing homosexuality, "I really appreciate you and value you as a person, but in all humility I believe that God has clearly said that homosexual practices are wrong and harmful to you." Postmodernists would say such a statement demonstrates bigotry and intolerance.

The Church is also under pressure to agree that all religions are equally valid. Christians do respect the right of individuals to make their own choices, but to say that all religious beliefs are of equal value is to demean God and His Word. In effect postmodernism says that all truth claims are equal—except those, like Christianity, that say that all truth claims are not equal. The one bigotry that seems to be acceptable is bigotry against Christians!

Pause for Thought

To what degree are you willing to compromise what you believe in order to gain the acceptance of others? What would the long-term cost be of such a compromise?

GOD'S WORD IS TRUE

God is the ultimate reality, and He is the truth. Logic and Christian faith are not incompatible. The rules of logic demonstrate the existence of a rational God who has revealed to humankind that which is true. Divine revelation is consistent with the natural sciences since God created all that is natural and left us with the ability to discover the natural laws that govern the universe. Consider the most important question facing everybody in the world: What happens when we die?

Hinduism teaches that when a soul dies it is reincarnated in another form. Christianity teaches that souls spend eternity in either heaven or hell. Atheists believe that we have no soul and that when we die, our existence simply ends. Postmodernism says that we can believe whatever we want to believe as long as we let others believe what they want to believe.

It is illogical to say that all of these beliefs are true. Does your belief about life after death make any difference to what will actually happen? Will all people everywhere have the same experience after death regardless of their beliefs? If Hindus are right, we will *all* be reincarnated. If Christians are right, we will *all* stand before the judgment seat of God. If atheists are right, our existence will come to an end. But it's illogical to believe that all of these beliefs are true.

There is only one logical conclusion: Truth exists regardless of what an individual chooses to believe. This is the view that Christians have held for thousands of years—a view that was taken as obvious until recently. Because God is truth, all genuine truth is God's truth and is true everywhere for everyone all the time. Truth is true in that it is objective and independent of any human perception. Because it is true, it cannot contradict itself.

Jesus said, "I am the way and the truth and the life; no one comes to the Father but through Me" (John 14:6). That is either a true statement or it isn't. Christians believe that Jesus is telling us the truth, but it upsets nonbelievers when we say there is only one way. The concept that every created thing works only one way is true in every other aspect of life. For instance, your computer will only work one way, which is the way the manufacturer designed it to work. You can try to use it your way, but it won't work. If you study the manufacturer's handbook, your computer can be a powerful tool. The same holds true for Christianity. God is the creator, and He gave us the Bible, which tells us why we are here, what happened after creation, why we are fallen creatures living in a fallen world and how we can be reestablished in a righteous relationship with Him. If we study His Word and live accordingly, we will bear much fruit and fulfill our purpose for being here.

Pause for Thought
If you stay committed to the truth, how can you do so without coming across as arrogant? If you disagree with someone's beliefs or actions, does it mean that you are also rejecting him or her as a person?

THE BIBLICAL WORLDVIEW

The worldviews of the nations in the Old Testament and of the Greek and Roman cultures in the New Testament are a combination of animism and polytheism (belief in many gods). Israel and the Early Church were constantly being challenged to follow other gods or philosophies, much as we are today. The apostle Paul warned us when he wrote Colossians 2:6-8:

Therefore as you have received Christ Jesus the Lord, so walk in Him, having been firmly rooted and now being built up in Him and established in your faith, just as you were instructed, and overflowing with gratitude. See to it that no one takes you captive through philosophy and empty deception, according to the tradition of men, according to the elementary principles of the world, rather than according to Christ.

The worldview taught by the true prophets and apostles is the one we need to know and believe. The biblical worldview has three functional realms: the realm of God, the realm of angels, and the realm of people and material things (see figure 4-C). These are not spatial realms but realms of being. God is not limited to a spatial realm existing far away in outer space. He is present everywhere in His creation and sustains all things by His power (see Hebrews 1:3). Jehovah God is the one and only being in the realm of deity—not God and angels, and certainly not God and Satan. Satan is a created being and does not possess the attributes of God. Satan is a fallen angel, and

Figure 4-C

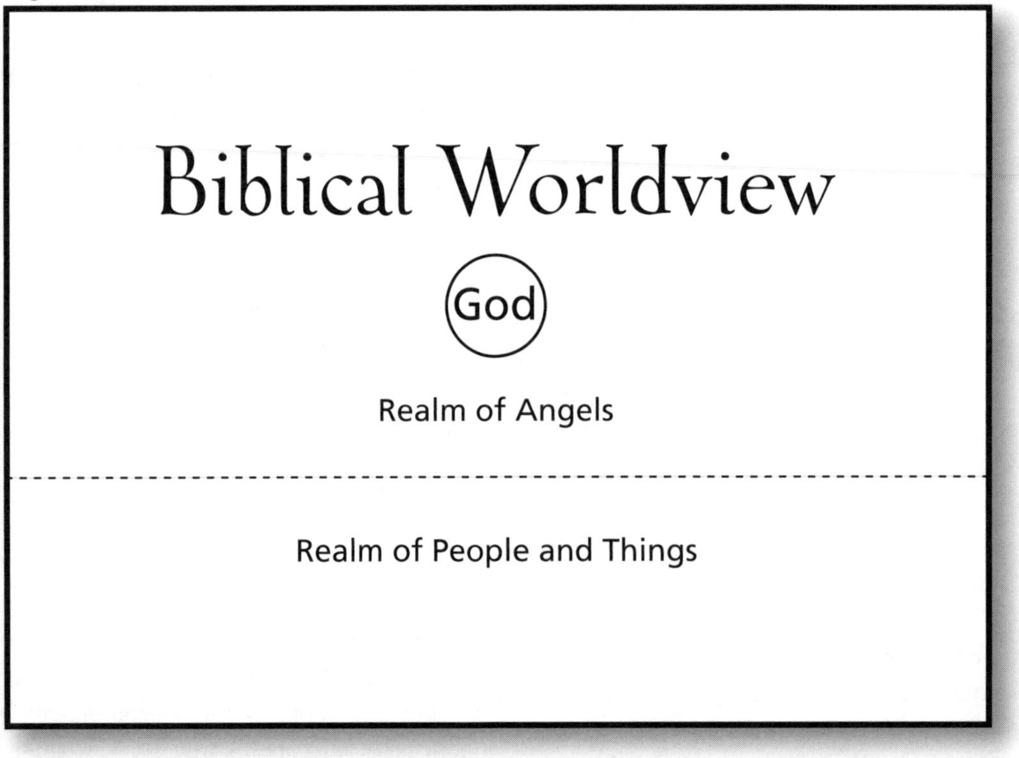

Biblical Worldview

(God)

Realm of Angels

- -

Realm of People and Things

when he rebelled against God, he was thrown out of heaven and took a third of the angels with him.

The realm of angels includes ministering spirits who are messengers of God. It also includes fallen angels, or demons, that are subject to Satan, the god of this fallen world. On Earth all three realms coexist and are operative. There is no spatial separation. God works through His angels and Church to build His kingdom. Satan works through his hierarchy of demons to perpetuate his kingdom of darkness. Every religious philosophy has detected the influence of God and the angelic realm. They attempt to define or manipulate the spiritual realm, but they lack any true perspective without divine revelation.

The eternal struggle is between good and evil: the kingdom of God and the kingdom of darkness, the Spirit of truth and the father of lies, between the true prophets and the false prophets, between angels and demons, between the Christ and the Antichrist. All believers are part of the battle whether they want to be or not. Paul taught that "our struggle is not against flesh and blood, but against the rulers, against the powers, against the world forces of this darkness, against the spiritual forces of darkness in the heavenly places [the spiritual realm]" (Ephesians 6:12).

Jesus did more than die for our sins and give us eternal life. He came to destroy the works of Satan (see 1 John 3:8). That is the gospel the animists are waiting to hear. They don't have to appease the deities, or try to manipulate the spiritual world through rituals and incantations. Satan has been disarmed. He is a defeated foe, and every believer has authority over the kingdom of darkness because of his or her position in Christ. That is just as much a part of the gospel as is forgiveness and new life in Christ.

Concerning our life before Christ, Paul wrote, "And you were dead in your trespasses and sins, in which you formerly walked according to the course of this world, according to the prince of the power of the air, of the spirit that is now working in the sons of disobedience" (Ephesians 2:1-2). Obviously, our worldview was not biblical before we came to Christ. So we need to renew our minds based on the truth of God's Word. Paul wrote, "And do not be conformed to this world, but be transformed by the renewing of your mind, so that you may prove what the will of God is, that which is good and acceptable and perfect" (Romans 12:2).

The Christian is called to believe and repent.

"Repent" literally means to change one's mind. Since our minds were shaped by this fallen world, we have to renew our minds to the truth of God's Word. Jesus said, "You will know the truth, and the truth will make you free. So if the Son makes you free, you will be free indeed" (John 8:32,36). Os Guinness wrote:

The Christian faith is not true because it works; it works because it is true. It is not true because we experience it; we experience it, deeply and gloriously, because it is true. It is not simply "true for us"; it is true for any who seek in order to find, because truth is true even if nobody believes it and falsehood is false even if everybody believes it. That is why truth does not yield to opinion, fashion, numbers, office or sincerity; it is simply true and that is the end of it.[2]

WITNESS

The following two questions will help participants begin to formulate ideas for sharing their faith with others. Invite volunteers to offer suggestions for witnessing to nonbelievers, and encourage participants to write down ideas in their student guide.

1. How will understanding that we all grow up with different worldviews help you talk to people who are not yet Christians?

2. What will you say to those who regard belief in absolute truth as being narrow-minded and bigoted?

GROUP DISCUSSION QUESTIONS

Instruct participants to form small groups of four to six, and assign each group several questions to discuss. Allow several minutes for discussion; then bring the whole group back together, and have volunteers from each small group share their group's questions and answers.

1. What was the worldview that you adopted as you were growing up?

2. Which worldview discussed in this session best describes the beliefs you held prior to coming to Christ?

3. Is your Christian worldview more valid or less valid than that of someone who grew up in another part of the world? Why?

4. What measure would you use to determine whether or not someone else's worldview is true?

5. When you make a stand for what you believe to be the truth, how can you do so without coming across as arrogant?

6. How can you disagree with someone's beliefs or actions without rejecting him or her as a person?

TAKING IT WITH YOU

The following information is included in the student guide and is intended for participants to use during the upcoming week. Direct participants to this section and encourage them to do the quiet-time suggestion and to consider the Big Question before the next session.

SUGGESTION FOR QUIET TIME

Ask the Holy Spirit to guide you into all truth and reveal to your mind the lies you have believed about the world in which we live.

THE BIG QUESTION

Before the next session, consider the following question:

Paul teaches that if believers live by the Spirit, they will not carry out the desires of the flesh (see Galatians 5:16). How do believers live by the Spirit?

Notes

1. Friedrich Nietzsche. *The Will to Power, Book III*, article 540.
   http://www.publicappeal.org/library/nietzsche/Nietzsche_the_will_to_power/the_will_to_power_book_III.htm (accessed February 5, 2004).
2. Os Guinness, *Time for Truth: Living Free in a World of Lies, Hype and Spin* (Grand Rapids, MI: Baker Books, 2000), p. 84.

LIVING BY THE SPIRIT

BUT I SAY, WALK BY THE SPIRIT, AND YOU WILL NOT CARRY OUT THE DESIRE OF THE FLESH.
FOR THE FLESH SETS ITS DESIRE AGAINST THE SPIRIT, AND THE SPIRIT AGAINST THE FLESH;
FOR THESE ARE IN OPPOSITION TO ONE ANOTHER, SO THAT YOU MAY NOT DO THE THINGS
THAT YOU PLEASE. BUT IF YOU ARE LED BY THE SPIRIT, YOU ARE NOT UNDER THE LAW.
GALATIANS 5:16-18

SESSION OVERVIEW

OBJECTIVE

In this session you will help participants understand what it means to live by the Spirit, avoiding both license and legalism, and by the grace of God, living a righteous life.

FOCUS TRUTH

When we become Christians, we are made new creations in Christ (see 2 Corinthians 5:17); however, we will still continue to struggle with our old sin nature. As Christians, we are no longer under the Law because the Law was a tutor to lead us to Christ. Christians can live a righteous life by believing what God says is true and by living in the power of the Holy Spirit.

BRIEFING

As Christians, we have a choice whether we will walk according to the flesh—our old way of thinking and behaving—or according to the Spirit.

It is important to understand that the terms "flesh," "self" and "nature" are *not* interchangeable. Some modern translations (e.g., the *New International Version*) interpret the Greek word *sarx* as "old nature" or "sinful nature," often adding the explanatory footnote "or flesh." In two significant places in the Bible the New Testament does use the Greek word *phusis*, meaning "nature." Ephesians 2:3 describes our nature before we came to Christ: "[We] were by nature children of wrath." In contrast, 2 Peter 1:4 reads that we now become "partakers of the divine nature"—we share God's nature (phusis) in our hearts—because new life in Christ means that we are united to Him.

Christians are no longer dead because of their sins. Christ dwells in us and makes us "alive because of righteousness" (Romans 8:10). The old self—who we were in Adam, or in the flesh—was "crucified with Christ" (Galatians 2:20). Once we accept Jesus Christ as our Savior, we are no longer in the flesh because we are in Christ. Every new creation in Christ has a new heart and a new spirit, thus a new core identity and nature that is directed toward God. However, the flesh remains and it has been conditioned to live independently of God. We can choose to live according to the flesh or according to the Spirit. The choice is ours to make.

LIVING BY THE SPIRIT

BUT I SAY, WALK BY THE SPIRIT, AND YOU WILL NOT CARRY OUT THE DESIRE OF THE FLESH.
FOR THE FLESH SETS ITS DESIRE AGAINST THE SPIRIT, AND THE SPIRIT AGAINST THE FLESH;
FOR THESE ARE IN OPPOSITION TO ONE ANOTHER, SO THAT YOU MAY NOT DO THE THINGS
THAT YOU PLEASE. BUT IF YOU ARE LED BY THE SPIRIT, YOU ARE NOT UNDER THE LAW.
GALATIANS 5:16-18

WELCOME

Welcome participants and open the meeting in prayer; then share the following story:

A young pilot had just passed the point of no return for his flight when the weather suddenly changed for the worse. Visibility dropped to a matter of feet as the clouds descended to Earth. Placing his trust in the cockpit instruments was a new experience for the pilot (for the ink was still wet on the certificate verifying that he was qualified for instrument flying), but it was the landing that worried him most. The destination for the flight was a crowded metropolitan airport—one that the pilot was not familiar with.

Alone with his thoughts until he could make radio contact with the airport's control tower, the young pilot was keenly aware how easily it would be to panic. After all, he was a new pilot, flying in bad weather with no visibility and heading toward a difficult landing. Twice, the pilot reached for the radio to broadcast a mayday call but instead forced himself to think about the flight manual his flight instructor had required all students to memorize. As a student, the young man did not care for having to memorize so much; however, as a pilot, he was now thankful he had been required to do so.

Finally, the voice of an air-traffic controller came on the radio. Trying not to sound apprehensive, the young pilot asked for landing instructions. "I'm going to put you on a holding pattern," the controller responded. *Great!* thought the pilot. *This guy will help me land safely.* Suddenly, the words of an old hymn popped into the pilot's mind: "Trust and obey for there's no other way" and took on new meaning. Aware that this was no time for pride, the pilot informed the controller, "This is not a seasoned pro up here. I would appreciate any help you could give me" and was relieved to hear "Roger that" in response.

For the next 45 minutes, the controller gently guided the pilot through the blinding fog. As periodic course and altitude corrections were given, the pilot realized the controller was guiding him around obstacles and away from potential collisions. With the words of the instruction book in his mind and the voice of the controller through his radio, the pilot was finally able to land his plane safely that stormy night.

WORSHIP

Spend a few minutes worshiping the Lord through prayer, song, praise or testimonies shared by volunteers.

WORD

 The Word section is available on the Beta DVD, or you can present the information yourself in a lecture format.

The Holy Spirit guides us through the maze of life much like the air-traffic controller in our story. The controller's guidance was based on the assumption that the pilot had an understanding of the instructions in his flight manual. Such is the case with the Holy Spirit—His guidance is dependent on our having the knowledge of God's Word established in our heart.

> But I say, walk by the Spirit, and you will not carry out the desire of the flesh. For the flesh sets its desire against the Spirit, and the Spirit against the flesh; for these are in opposition to one another, so that you may not do the things that you please. But if you are led by the Spirit, you are not under the Law (Galatians 5:16-18).

As believers, we are new creations in Christ. The Holy Spirit has taken up residence in our lives, and we have become partakers of God's divine nature—we have been given a new heart and a new spirit.

Paul wrote in Galatians 5:17 that the flesh and the Spirit are in opposition to each other. As Christians living in this fallen world, we can choose to walk either according to the Spirit or according to the flesh. Our countenance and behavior will reflect our choice.

Pause for Thought
What best characterizes your life—the deeds of the flesh or the fruit of the Spirit?

WALKING BY THE SPIRIT

How then do we live, or walk, by the Spirit? If we were to answer this question with three steps and a formula, we'd be putting Christians back under the law! To walk by the Spirit is not a legal issue—it's a personal one.

What Walking by the Spirit Is *Not*

In order to understand what walking by the Spirit is, let's take a look at Galatians 5:16-18, which explains what walking by the Spirit is *not*. When we understand what it is not, we can identify parameters within which we are to live.

1. **Walking by the Spirit is not license.** "License" can be defined as an excessive or undisciplined lifestyle that constitutes the abuse of a privilege. To be licentious means that one lacks moral discipline and has no regard for accepted rules and regulations. This passage teaches that if we walk by the

Spirit, we won't carry out the desires of the flesh, and we won't do whatever we please.

Paul wrote, "For you were called to freedom, brethren; only do not turn your freedom into an opportunity for the flesh, but through love serve one another" (Galatians 5:13). Each of us is free by the grace of God to live a responsible life. Just as good parents set parameters within which their children can learn and grow in safety, God has also provided protective commandments under which we are to live. Now that we are children of God, the presence of the Holy Spirit convicts us when we try to live according to the flesh or outside the parameters God has given us. Imagine if the air-traffic controller had said to the young pilot, "Go ahead and land whenever you want. Pick a spot and go for it!" There is little doubt the pilot would have been in big trouble. If there were no moral restraints and boundaries to govern our behavior as Christians, we would find ourselves in a freefall straight into moral decadence.

If we choose to walk by the flesh, we will have to live with the negative consequences that come from making bad choices. Living by the Spirit, however, has no negative consequences.

2. **Walking by the Spirit is not legalism.** "But now we have been released from the Law, having died to that by which we were bound, so that we serve in newness of the Spirit and not in oldness of the letter" (Romans 7:6). God has called us to live righteous lives, but we cannot do that by living under the Law. There are three reasons for this.

- **The Law commonly produces guilt.** (See Galatians 3:10-14.) When Adam and Eve sinned they lost their relationship with God. Part of God's plan to redeem fallen humanity was to establish a conditional covenant with His people. Through Moses, God gave us the Law—a moral standard of righteousness. Without a righteousness standard, there is no sin.

  Nobody could live up to the standard set by the Law, which was part of His plan. The Law was a tutor to lead us to Christ (see Galatians 3:24). It showed us our sin and our need for a Savior. Paul wrote, "Cursed is everyone who does not abide by all things written in the Book of the Law . . . that no one is justified by the

Law before God is evident; for 'the righteous man shall live by faith'" (vv. 10-11). On the contrary, "He who practices them will live by them" (v. 12). "Cursed is everyone who hangs on a tree" (v. 13)—Jesus Christ redeemed us by satisfying the just demands of the Law, that "the blessing given to Abraham might come to the Gentiles, so that we would receive the promise of the Spirit through faith" (v. 14). We are not saved by how we perform; we are saved and sanctified by what we have chosen to believe.

James 2:10 reads: "For whoever keeps the whole law and yet stumbles in one point, he has become guilty of all." Thankfully, our relationship with God is based on His grace and not on our ability to keep the Law. Every born-again believer is forgiven, alive and free in Christ—and no longer under the old covenant of Law.

- **The Law is powerless to give life.** Telling people that what they are doing is wrong does not give them the power to stop doing it. Paul wrote, "Is the Law then contrary to the promises of God? May it never be! For if a law had been given which was able to impart life, then righteousness would indeed have been based on law" (Galatians 3:21).

  Paul explained that we are "servants of a new covenant, not of the letter [of the Law] but of the Spirit; for the letter kills, but the Spirit gives life" (2 Corinthians 3:6). Christians live righteous lives by faith in the power of the Holy Spirit.

- **The Law has the capacity to stimulate the desire to do that which it was intended to prohibit.** Simply laying down the law can actually arouse our sinful passions. Paul warned about this in Romans 7:5: "For while we were in the flesh, the sinful passions, which were aroused by the Law, were at work in the members of our body to bear fruit for death." Does this mean the law is sinful?

What shall we say then? Is the Law sin? May it never be! On the contrary, I would not have come to know sin except through the Law; for I would not have known about coveting if the Law had not said, "You shall not covet." But sin, taking opportunity through the commandment, produced in me coveting of every kind; for apart from the Law sin is dead (Romans 7:7-8).

The moment a parent tells a child where he or she *cannot* go, where does that child desperately want to go? Exactly the place from which he or she has been forbidden. What is forbidden can seem most desirable.

Of course, this doesn't mean that we don't need or shouldn't have a moral standard. Without a moral standard, we wouldn't come to Christ. But now that we are in Christ, the Law is no longer the means by which we live *righteous lives*. The Holy Spirit will guide us to live between the two extremes of legalism and license.

Share the following illustration:

The Christian life is like a journey up a narrow mountain path, with the Holy Spirit offering sanctuary to those who stay on the path. To the right of the path is a steep cliff that promises an exhilarating, albeit temporary, flight. It can be tempting to give in to the desires of the flesh and demand your *right* to freedom of choice—to take license with the free will you've been given. But ignoring the consequence will not lessen it, and you will no doubt have a rude awakening when the ground rushes up to meet you at the end of your flight.

To the left of the path is a roaring fire. The "accuser of our brethren" (Revelation 12:10) is just waiting to have a field day with those who choose to deviate from the path and go back to the law. Many are burned by legalism. Some who fall into this trap become perfectionists, trying desperately to live up to the law; others feel so condemned by their failures that they stay away from churches and friends for fear that they will be made to feel guilty. Paul wrote, "It was for freedom that Christ set us free; therefore keep standing firm and do not be subject again to a yoke of slavery" (Galatians 5:1).

The devil is both the tempter on the cliff and the accuser by the fire. He wants us to jump off the cliff and taunts us: "Go on and do it. Everybody is doing it. You will get away with it. Who would know? You know you want to." As soon as we give in to the temptation, his role changes from tempter to accuser: "You're sick. And you call yourself a Christian. You will never get away with this. God can't possibly love such a miserable failure as you."

What Walking by the Spirit *Is*

If walking by the Spirit is not license, and it's not legalism, then what is it? It is *liberty*. "Now the Lord is the Spirit, and where the Spirit of the Lord is, there is liberty" (2 Corinthians 3:17). Let's consider how we can experience this liberated walk with God.

Pause for Thought
Which have you struggled with more—license or legalism?

WALKING WITH GOD

Before we can say that we have an understanding of what it means to live free in Christ, we must understand that living by the Spirit is not sitting passively, expecting God to do everything for us—and neither is it running around in endless, exhausting activities as though everything depends on our efforts.

Jesus said that apart from Him we "can do nothing" (John 15:5). Not much is accomplished in the kingdom of God if we expect God to do everything without us. It is the eternal purpose of God to make His wisdom known through the Church (see Ephesians 3:8-11). At the same time, not much gets accomplished for the kingdom of God if we try to do it all by ourselves.

Take Up His Yoke

Responding to pharisaic legalism, Jesus said, "Come to Me all who are weary and heavy-laden, and I will give you rest. Take My yoke upon you and learn from Me, for I am gentle and humble in heart, and you will find rest for your souls. For My yoke is easy and My burden is light" (Matthew 11:28-30). Why did Jesus use this terminology?

Jesus, a carpenter by trade, understood not only how to make a yoke but also its important purpose. When

the time came for a young ox to be trained, its master would harness it to a lead ox using a yoke. The lead ox knew that the best way to accomplish a full day's work was to walk a steady, even pace, looking neither to the left nor the right. Sometimes, a younger, untrained ox would get impatient and want to run ahead of the lead ox, only to get a sore neck for all its effort. Other times, the young ox might decide it didn't want to work and would try to sit down. What would it get? A sore neck! In either case, the lead ox would keep right on with its slow and steady pace because it had been trained to listen to its master.

We are just like the young oxen; whether we sit down or drop out, life goes on. When we are yoked with Jesus, He will maintain a steady pace right down the center of that narrow path, where our walk is one of faith and not of sight, and one of grace and not legalism. When we look at our lives in retrospect, we can say "I did this and I did that. I went here and I went there"—but how much fruit remains? Our activities are not a measure of our spirituality; our spirituality is measured by the fruit of righteousness and reproduction.

Jesus said, "I am gentle and humble in heart" (Matthew 11:29). This passage in Matthew is the only place in the New Testament where Jesus described Himself. We have been invited to walk with the gentle Jesus. Imagine that! "Therefore as you have received Christ Jesus the Lord, so walk in Him" (Colossians 2:6).

Follow His Lead

Being led by the Spirit is defined by two parameters. First, the Holy Spirit is not pushing us. Many Christians are motivated by guilt and have a hard time saying no. These Christians expend a lot of energy but bear very little fruit. Driven people measure success by the number of activities they are involved in and measure spirituality by the expenditure of human energy. There is a major difference between being called into ministry and being driven to perform. The latter leads to burnout.

Second, we are never lured away by the Holy Spirit. If we are being pressured to make a hasty decision, we should simply refuse because God doesn't lead that way—the devil does. He demands an immediate answer and withdraws the offer if time for consideration is requested. The guidance of God may come suddenly, but it never comes to the spiritually unprepared. This was demonstrated at Pentecost; it was sudden, but the disciples had spent days in prayerful preparation.

The lure of knowledge and power is the most common trap believers fall into, but the truth is that we already have all the power we need in Christ (see Ephesians 1:18-19), and the Holy Spirit will lead us into all truth. Some are easily lured away because they have not exercised any spiritual discipline, such as Bible study and prayer. These Christians are like pilots who want the air-traffic controller to explain the instruction manual to them while they are in the air.

Share the following personal story from Neil Anderson:

Growing up on a farm, I had the privilege of raising champion-stock sheep. I can tell you from experience that sheep are not the smartest animals on the farm. They're right up there with chickens. For instance, you can self-feed cattle and pigs, but not sheep. If you turn sheep loose in a green pasture without a shepherd, they will literally eat themselves to death. I believe that is why the shepherd "makes me lie down in green pastures" (Psalm 23:2).

In the Western world, we drive sheep from the rear, much like the Australians who use sheepdogs. However, that is not the case in Israel. During my trips to the Holy Land, I observed shepherds sitting patiently while the flock fed on the grass. When an area was sufficiently grazed, the shepherd would say something and walk off. The sheep looked up and followed him. What a beautiful illustration of what the Lord said in John 10:27, "My sheep hear My voice, and I know them, and they follow Me."

Walking by the Spirit is neither license nor legalism. It's not sitting passively, waiting for God to do something; nor is it running around in endless activities, trying to accomplish something by our own strength and resources. If we walk by the Spirit, we are neither driven nor lured off the path of faith. "For all who are being led by the Spirit of God, these are sons of God" (Romans 8:14).

WITNESS

The following question will help participants begin to formulate ideas for sharing their faith with others.

Invite volunteers to offer suggestions for witnessing to nonbelievers, and encourage participants to write down ideas in their student guide. Also, encourage them to elaborate on their ideas with specific examples.

How can being led by the Holy Spirit affect your witness?

GROUP DISCUSSION QUESTIONS

Instruct participants to form small groups of four to six, and assign each group several questions to discuss. Allow several minutes for discussion; then bring the whole group back together, and have volunteers from each small group share their group's questions and answers.

1. What were the key elements ensuring the safe landing of the young pilot in the opening illustration?

   a. Knowledge of _____

   b. Faith in _____

2. Why has simply preaching morality not changed our society?

3. What does legalism accomplish, and why is the law ineffective?

4. Has the laying down of the law in your church, home or society ever stimulated you to do what the law is intended to prohibit? Explain.

5. Which side of the road (the cliff or the fire) represents your greater weakness (license or legalism)? How can you stay in the center of the road?

6. What would you learn if you walked with Jesus?

7. How did Jesus describe Himself?

8. How does the Holy Spirit's guidance come or not come, and who can expect to be guided?

9. What steps can you take to be more sensitive to the Holy Spirit's guidance in your life?

TAKING IT WITH YOU

The following information is included in the student guide and is intended for participants to use during the upcoming week. Direct participants to this section and encourage them to do the quiet-time suggestion and to consider the Big Question before the next session.

SUGGESTION FOR QUIET TIME

Begin each day by asking your heavenly Father to fill you with His Holy Spirit, and commit yourself to living by faith in the power of the Holy Spirit.

THE BIG QUESTION

Before the next session, consider the following question:

Since you are a new creation in Christ, why do you still struggle with the same old thoughts and habits?

RENEWING THE MIND

FOR THOUGH WE WALK IN THE FLESH, WE DO NOT WAR ACCORDING TO THE FLESH,
FOR THE WEAPONS OF OUR WARFARE ARE NOT OF THE FLESH, BUT DIVINELY POW-
ERFUL FOR THE DESTRUCTION OF FORTRESSES. WE ARE DESTROYING SPECULATIONS
AND EVERY LOFTY THING RAISED UP AGAINST THE KNOWLEDGE OF GOD, AND WE
ARE TAKING EVERY THOUGHT CAPTIVE TO THE OBEDIENCE OF CHRIST.
2 CORINTHIANS 10:3-5

SESSION OVERVIEW

OBJECTIVE

In this session, you will help participants understand how mental strongholds, or flesh patterns, are formed and how they can be torn down in Christ.

FOCUS TRUTH

When we come into this world, we have neither the presence of God in our lives nor the knowledge of His ways. So we learn how to live our lives independently of God. In order to grow, we have to be transformed by the renewing of our minds.

BRIEFING

Mental strongholds are sometimes called flesh patterns and are similar to what psychologists call defense mechanisms. They are habitual thought patterns. In this session we want to help people understand what mental strongholds are and how they are formed. During this session we will mention the Steps to Freedom in Christ (the Steps), which is a repentance process that the group will go through in a later session. The Steps will help participants resolve their personal and spiritual conflicts by submitting to God and resisting the devil.

RENEWING THE MIND

FOR THOUGH WE WALK IN THE FLESH, WE DO NOT WAR ACCORDING TO THE FLESH, FOR THE WEAPONS OF OUR WARFARE ARE NOT OF THE FLESH, BUT DIVINELY POWERFUL FOR THE DESTRUCTION OF FORTRESSES. WE ARE DESTROYING SPECULATIONS AND EVERY LOFTY THING RAISED UP AGAINST THE KNOWLEDGE OF GOD, AND WE ARE TAKING EVERY THOUGHT CAPTIVE TO THE OBEDIENCE OF CHRIST.

2 CORINTHIANS 10:3-5

WELCOME

Welcome participants and open the meeting in prayer. Ask for a show of hands for those who have tried walking by the Spirit since the last session. Invite volunteers to share their answers to why Christians continue to struggle after becoming new creations in Christ. After several have shared, read the following illustration:

Slavery in the United States was abolished by the Thirteenth Amendment on December 18, 1865. How many slaves were there on December 19? In reality, none, but many still lived like slaves because they never learned the truth. Others heard the good news but continued living as they had always been taught and thus maintained their negative self-image.

The plantation owners were devastated by this proclamation of emancipation. *We're ruined! Slavery has been abolished. We've lost the battle to keep our slaves.* But their chief spokesman slyly responded, "Not necessarily. As long as these people think they're still slaves, the proclamation of emancipation will have no practical effect. We don't have any legal right over them anymore, but many don't know it. Keep your slaves from learning the truth, and your control over them will not even be challenged."

But what if the news spreads? "Don't panic. We have another barrel on our gun. We may not be able to keep them from hearing the news; we still have the potential to deceive the whole world. They don't call me the father of lies for nothing. Just tell them that they misunderstood the Thirteenth Amendment. Tell them that they

are going to be free, not that they are free already. The truth they heard is just positional truth, not actual truth. Someday they may receive the benefits, but not yet."

But they'll expect us to say that. They won't believe us. "Then pick out a few persuasive ones who are convinced that they're still slaves, and let them do the talking for you. Remember, most of these newly freed people were born slaves and have lived like slaves all their lives. All we have to do is to deceive them so that they still think like slaves. As long as they continue doing what slaves do, it will not be hard to convince them that they must still be slaves. They will maintain their slave identity because of the things they do. The moment they try to confess that they are no longer slaves, just whisper in their ears, 'How can you even think you are no longer a slave when you are doing things that slaves do?' After all, we also have the capacity to accuse the brethren day and night."

Years later, many slaves still had not heard the wonderful news that they had been freed, so naturally they continued to live the way they had always lived. Some slaves had heard the good news, but they evaluated it by what they were presently doing and feeling. They reasoned, *I'm still living in bondage, doing the same things I have always done. My experience tells me that I must not be free. I'm feeling the same way I was before the proclamation, so it must not be true. After all, your feelings always tell the truth.* So they continued to live according to how they felt, not wanting to be hypocrites.

One former slave heard the good news, and received it with great joy. He checked out the validity of the proclamation and found out that the highest of all authorities originated the decree. Not only that, but it personally cost that authority a tremendous price which he willingly paid so that the slaves could be free. As a result, the slave's life was transformed. He correctly reasoned that it would be hypocritical to believe his feelings and not the truth. Determined to live by what he knows to be true, his experience began to change rather dramatically. He realized that his old master had no authority over him and did not need to be obeyed. He gladly served the one who set him free.[1]

WORSHIP

Spend a few minutes worshiping the Lord through prayer, song, praise or testimonies shared by volunteers.

WORD

 The Word section is available on the Beta DVD, or you can present the information yourself in a lecture format.

RENEWING THE MIND

Our good news has not been kept from us. We are no longer slaves to sin because we are bond servants of Christ. So then, if this is true—and it is—why don't we feel much different from the way we felt before we received Christ, and why are we still struggling with the same issues we struggled with before we became Christians?

Let's take a look at the bigger picture: In session 1 of this course, we discovered that it was because of the Fall that we are all born physically alive but spiritually dead in our trespasses and sins (see Ephesians 2:1). During our early formative years—before we knew the truth about Jesus Christ—we learned how to live our lives independently of God. Once we accepted Jesus into our hearts, we were born again—new creations in Christ. This is wonderful; however, everything that was previously programmed into our memory banks is still

there. That is why Paul wrote, "And do not be conformed to this world, but be transformed by the renewing of your mind, so that you may prove what the will of God is, that which is good and acceptable and perfect" (Romans 12:2).

Share Neil Anderson's naval experience:

It is customary in the United States Navy to refer to the captain of the ship as the "old man." The first captain I had was a lousy old man. He belittled his officers and drank excessively with the senior enlisted men. If I was going to survive on board that ship, I had to learn how to cope and defend myself under his authority. One day he got transferred off the ship; he was gone forever, and I wasn't under his authority anymore. We got a new captain, and he was a good one. But how do you think I continued to live on board that ship? I lived the way I was trained under the previous captain until I got to know the new one. I began to slowly realize that my old means of coping weren't necessary any more—just as when I became a Christian, I had to learn a new way to live under the authority of my new captain, the Lord Jesus Christ.

We are no longer under the authority of the god of this world. We are children of God. Our greatest priority is to get to know this new captain of our souls. The apostle Paul wrote, "I count all things to be loss in view of the surpassing value of knowing Christ Jesus my Lord" (Philippians 3:8).

Pause for Thought
How do you think having an abusive father could distort your feelings toward your heavenly Father?

MAJOR CONTRIBUTING FACTORS TO STRONGHOLDS

Our temperaments have been shaped by mental strongholds. It will take time to renew our minds, and to replace the lies we have believed with the truth of

God's Word. There are two major factors that contribute to the formation of these strongholds.

Prevailing Experiences

There is general agreement that our worldview and attitudes are primarily assimilated from the environment in which we were raised. A major part of this programming took place in our early childhood through prevailing experiences (e.g., the families we were raised in, the churches we attended or didn't attend, the neighborhood and communities we grew up in, the friends that we had or didn't have) and how we responded to our environment. Two children can be raised in the same home, have the same parents, eat the same food, have similar friends, go to the same church, and each responds differently to circumstances throughout his or her life. Remember Jacob and Esau?! We all interpret the world in which we live differently. In addition, God created us uniquely in our mother's womb; He has known us since the foundation of the world (see Psalm 139:13,15-16).

Traumatic Experiences

The second greatest contributor to the development of mental strongholds is traumatic experiences. These experiences have been burned into our minds suddenly due to their intensity. Such trauma could include rape, divorce and death. Unfortunately, our traumatic experiences have been filed away in our memories, and there is no delete button in our organic computer (aka our brain).

As we struggle to reprogram our minds against the lies we have believed due to our traumatic experiences, we are also confronted daily with an ungodly world system. Even Christians can continue to allow the world to affect their minds. This is why Paul warned us to "not be conformed to this world" (Romans 12:2). He also cautioned us to "see to it that no one takes you captive through philosophy and empty deception, according to the tradition of men, according to the elementary principles of the world, rather than according to Christ" (Colossians 2:8).

The good news is that we have all the resources that we need to renew our minds. The Lord has sent the Holy Spirit, the Spirit of truth, to guide us into all truth (see John 16:13). Because we are one with God, "we have the mind of Christ" (1 Corinthians 2:16). We have

superior weapons to win the battle for our minds according to Paul in 2 Corinthians 10:3-5:

> For though we walk in the flesh, we do not war according to the flesh, for the weapons of our warfare are not of the flesh, but divinely powerful for the destruction of fortresses. We are destroying speculations and every lofty thing raised up against the knowledge of God, and we are taking every thought captive to the obedience of Christ.

Paul is not talking about defensive armor; he's talking about battering-ram weaponry that tears down strongholds that have been raised up against the knowledge of God.

Temptation

Since we live in this world, we will continuously face temptation. We are assured, however, that we are not alone in this.

> No temptation has overtaken you but such as is common to man; and God is faithful, who will not allow you to be tempted beyond what you are able, but with the temptation will provide the way of escape also, so that you will be able to endure it (1 Corinthians 10:13).

It's not a sin to be tempted. If that were the case, then the worst sinner who ever lived would be Jesus because He "has been tempted in all things as we are, yet without sin" (Hebrews 4:15).

Satan knows exactly which buttons to push in each of us! He knows our every weakness and our entire family history. Things that tempt one person may not tempt another. Every temptation is an attempt by Satan to get us to live our lives independently of God, to walk according to the flesh rather than according to the Spirit. When faced with the temptation to turn a rock into bread to satisfy His hunger, Jesus said, "It is written, 'Man shall not live on bread alone, but on every word that proceeds out of the mouth of God'" (Matthew 4:4). The devil wanted Jesus to use His divine attributes independent of the Father.

Temptation begins with a seed thought in our minds; and unless we take our thoughts captive, we will eventually allow them to lead us to sin. Share the following example:

Suppose a man is struggling with alcoholism and pornography. One night his wife asks him to go to the store for some milk. When he gets in his car, he wrestles for a brief moment with whether to buy the milk from the local grocery store or the convenience store down the street. He decides to go to the convenience store, knowing that liquor and pornography are sold there. As soon as the man begins driving toward the convenience store, the battle for his mind is lost. He begins to rationalize his decision. *The convenience store is a block closer, and with gas prices the way they are, every block counts! Besides, if God doesn't want me to go there, He'll cause a wreck at the intersection, and I'll just head toward the grocery store.* As he reaches the convenience store parking lot, his mind continues, *If you don't want me to buy any booze or look at the pornography, Lord, have my pastor be at the store buying milk.*

The undisciplined mind can rationalize poor choices, but the rationalization doesn't last. Before he has even left the store, guilt and shame overwhelm the man who was sent to buy milk. The tempter now becomes the accuser, taunting the man with thoughts such as *You sick person, when are you going to get over this? How can you call yourself a Christian?*

Habit

Suppose we consciously make a choice to give in to the temptation. If we continue to act on that choice, we will establish a habit in about six weeks. If the habit persists, a stronghold will develop in our minds, becoming evident in our temperaments and in the way we live.

If we don't take that first thought captive in obedience to Christ, we will respond emotionally to our thoughts. Our feelings are primarily a product of our thought life. The tendency is to believe that something or somebody has made us feel a certain way, but that really isn't true. All external data is processed by our minds—over which we have complete control. It would logically follow that our feelings can be distorted by what we *choose* to think or believe, and if what we choose to believe does not reflect truth, then what we feel will not reflect reality.

EXAMPLES OF STRONGHOLDS

As we've already discussed, mental strongholds are sometimes called flesh patterns and are similar to what psychologists call defense mechanisms. There are an infinite number of potential combinations that can make up strongholds. Let's consider just a few.

Inferiority

The issue of inferiority is common even among Christians. An inferiority complex is not formed overnight; it happens over time to people raised in a performance-based environment—which is the case for almost everyone. No matter how hard we try, we will never be able to live up to everyone else's expectations. When we continue to strive for the elusive acceptance that never comes, we begin to struggle with a sense of inferiority because there will always be someone who is stronger, smarter or better looking than we are.

Pause for Thought
Secular counselors know that their clients struggle with low self-worth, but how might their solution to this issue differ from that of a Christian counselor?

Homosexuality

Those who are caught in the stronghold of homosexuality weren't born that way. Because of the Fall, a person can be genetically predisposed to certain strengths and weaknesses, but that does not make a person homosexual from birth. Homosexuality is a false identity with which we have labeled ourselves or others. There is no such thing as a homosexual. There are homosexual thoughts, feelings and behaviors, and the latter is what the Lord condemns. Heaping condemnation upon those who struggle in this way will prove counterproductive. People who are caught in this stronghold already suffer from an incredible identity crisis, and overbearing authoritarianism is what drove many to this lifestyle in the first place.

Most people who struggle with homosexual tendencies or behaviors have had poor developmental upbringing. Sexual abuse, dysfunctional families in which the roles of mom and dad are reversed, exposure to homosexual literature prior to fully developing a sexual identity, playground teasing and poor relationships with the opposite sex all contribute to mental and emotional development. The events that precipitated these mental and emotional difficulties have to be resolved, and the mind must be reprogrammed with the truth of God's Word.

Sometimes it is difficult to find a precipitating event in the life of someone caught in this lifestyle. How then do we explain the development of this stronghold? Suppose a young man looks at another man in a locker room at school and has a tempting thought. That is all it is, just a tempting thought, and he may dismiss it the first time. Then it happens again and again, so he begins to think, *Why do I keep thinking about that guy in this way? Maybe I'm homosexual.* The sexual stronghold becomes entrenched the moment he believes that lie. Instead of taking every thought captive to the obedience of Christ, he lets his mind dwell on sexual thoughts. This, as we've already discussed, will eventually affect his feelings, which will then cause him to physically involve himself with another man; and the end result is that sin will reign in his mortal body, because he has used his body as an instrument of unrighteousness (see Romans 6:12).

Pause for Thought
How can a Christian keep his or her mind pure when pornography is so prevalent?

Alcoholism

Adult children of alcoholics tend to struggle with this stronghold. Suppose three boys were raised by a father who became addicted to alcohol after years of drinking. The older boy believed that he was strong enough to stand up to Dad. There was no way he was going to take anything from this drunk. The middle boy didn't believe he could stand up to Dad, so he accommodated him instead. The youngest boy was terrorized. When Dad came home, the boy headed for the closet or hid under the bed. Twenty years later, the father is gone. These three boys are now adults. When they are confronted with a hostile situation, how will they respond? The older one will fight, the middle one will accommodate and the younger one will run and hide. Those are mental strongholds.

In Romans 6:11, Paul reminds us that we are to consider ourselves dead to sin and alive to God in Christ Jesus. As Christians our relationship with sin is over, but sin is still present and appealing. We can choose to sin, but we don't *have* to. It is our responsibility to not let sin reign in our mortal bodies. Confession alone will not resolve that. It takes complete repentance.

Later in this course, we will be going through the Steps, a repentance process that helps us submit to God and resist the devil. None of us will be embarrassed because it is essentially an issue between each of us and God. While going through the Steps, we will be guided by the Holy Spirit into truth and that truth will set us free. To overcome the sin that wages war in our members, we have to renounce the unrighteous use of our bodies, submit them to God as living sacrifices and be transformed by the renewing of our minds.

WITNESS

The following two questions will help participants begin to formulate ideas for sharing their faith with others. Invite volunteers to offer suggestions for witnessing to nonbelievers, and encourage participants to write down ideas in their student guide.

1. Knowing that people have certain mind-sets because of their upbringing, how might this help or hinder your witness to them?

2. Since people are in bondage to the lies they have believed, what hope could you extend to them?

GROUP DISCUSSION QUESTIONS

Instruct participants to form small groups of four to six, and assign each group several questions to discuss. Allow several minutes for discussion; then bring the whole group back together, and have volunteers from each small group share their group's questions and answers.

1. Why don't all Christians think the same?

2. How do mental strongholds develop?

3. Share an example of how believing a lie has affected how people feel about God or someone else. Can you give a personal example?

4. How can Christians stand up against temptation?

5. Why must you choose to believe what God says is true even when it doesn't feel true?

6. Explain why born-again believers may not feel saved or feel that God loves them.

TAKING IT WITH YOU

The following information is included in the student guide and is intended for participants to use during the upcoming week. Direct participants to this section and encourage them to do the quiet-time suggestion and to consider the Big Question before the next session.

SUGGESTION FOR QUIET TIME

During the coming week, take time each day to meditate on the following Scripture passages:

- Romans 8:31-39

- Ephesians 1:1-19

- Philippians 4:12-13

THE BIG QUESTION

Before the next session, consider the following question:

How can Satan deceive you?

Note
1. Neil T. Anderson and Robert L. Saucy, *God's Power at Work in You* (Eugene, OR: Harvest House, 2001), pp. 25-27.

THE BATTLE FOR THE MIND

PUT ON THE FULL ARMOR OF GOD, SO THAT YOU WILL BE ABLE TO STAND FIRM
AGAINST THE SCHEMES OF THE DEVIL. FOR OUR STRUGGLE IS NOT AGAINST FLESH AND
BLOOD, BUT AGAINST THE RULERS, AGAINST THE POWERS, AGAINST THE WORLD FORCES
OF THIS DARKNESS, AGAINST THE SPIRITUAL FORCES OF WICKEDNESS IN THE HEAVENLY
PLACES. THEREFORE, TAKE UP THE FULL ARMOR OF GOD, SO THAT YOU WILL BE ABLE
TO RESIST IN THE EVIL DAY, AND HAVING DONE EVERYTHING, TO STAND FIRM
EPHESIANS 6:11-13

SESSION OVERVIEW

OBJECTIVE

In this session, you will help participants understand the spiritual battle for their minds so that mental strongholds, or defense mechanisms, can be replaced with God's truth and every thought taken captive to the obedience of Christ.

FOCUS TRUTH

We as believers have to renew our minds because we have been programmed to live independently from God. Even after salvation, flesh patterns remain and there is a constant spiritual battle for our minds. These mental strongholds must be torn down in Christ.

BRIEFING

Because of the nature of the information in this session, you may experience more than the typical amount of questions; and because issues may surface that participants have not yet dealt with, you may also be asked for help after the session. You are unmasking Satan's schemes, and it is important to pray in the meeting room before you start. Exercise the spiritual authority you have in Christ and commit yourself, the room and all the equipment you will be using during this session to the Lord. Ask for God's protection over yourself and over the hearts and minds of every participant.

THE BATTLE FOR THE MIND

PUT ON THE FULL ARMOR OF GOD, SO THAT YOU WILL BE ABLE TO STAND FIRM AGAINST THE SCHEMES OF THE DEVIL. FOR OUR STRUGGLE IS NOT AGAINST FLESH AND BLOOD, BUT AGAINST THE RULERS, AGAINST THE POWERS, AGAINST THE WORLD FORCES OF THIS DARKNESS, AGAINST THE SPIRITUAL FORCES OF WICKEDNESS IN THE HEAVENLY PLACES. THEREFORE, TAKE UP THE FULL ARMOR OF GOD, SO THAT YOU WILL BE ABLE TO RESIST IN THE EVIL DAY, AND HAVING DONE EVERYTHING, TO STAND FIRM.

EPHESIANS 6:11-13

WELCOME

Welcome participants and invite a volunteer to open the meeting in prayer; then ask for a show of hands to see how many in the group would be open to having all of their thoughts put up on a screen for everyone to see. Don't wait too long for hands to go up—you might be waiting all night! The tendency is to think that we are the only ones who struggle with bad thoughts, but the truth is, we all struggle with them. What if all those thoughts didn't originate from you, and you could get rid of them? Then you could have mental peace! Is that possible? Would you like to have that? You can be mentally and emotionally free as the result of genuine repentance.

Share the following letter Neil Anderson received from a woman who had completed the Steps to Freedom in Christ. (We have omitted personal information to protect the privacy of the author of the letter.)

I would like to share an entry I made in my journal Sunday night after our meeting on Friday.

"Since Friday afternoon I have felt like a different person. The fits of rage and anger are gone. My spirit is so calm and full of joy . . . I wake up singing praise to God in my heart. That edge of tension and irritation is gone. The Bible has been really exciting, stimulating and more understanding than ever before. There was nothing dramatic that happened during the session on Friday, yet I know in the deepest part of my being that something has changed. I am no longer bound by accusations, doubts, and thoughts of suicide or murder or other harm that came straight from hell into my head. There is a serenity in my mind and spirit, a clarity of consciousness that is profound.

"I'm excited and expectant about my future now. I know that I'll be growing spiritually again, and will be developing in other ways as well. I look forward happily to the discovery of the person God has created and redeemed, as well as the transformation of my marriage. It is so wonderful to have joy after so long a darkness."

It has been over two months since I wrote that, and I'm firmly convinced of the significant benefits of finding our freedom in Christ. I've been in therapy for months, but there is no comparison with the steps I am able to make now. Not only is my spirit more serene, my head is actually clearer. It is easier to make connections and integrate things now. It seems like everything is easier to understand now.

WORSHIP

Spend a few minutes worshiping the Lord through prayer, song, praise or testimonies shared by volunteers.

WORD

 The Word section is available on the Beta DVD, or you can present the information yourself in a lecture format.

We have learned how living in this fallen world has shaped our thinking, and how, before knowing Christ, our minds were programmed to live independently of God. There are all kinds of mixed messages in this world. Consequently, there are a lot of mixed emotions. There are Christians who don't feel saved, who don't feel like God loves them, who don't feel like they're worth anything. Previous messages they received weren't true, but they believed them nonetheless, resulting in irresponsible behavior and troubled emotions. However, Scripture clearly teaches that not all the messages we receive are from the world: "But the Spirit explicitly says that in later times some will fall away from the faith, paying attention to deceitful spirits and doctrines of demons" (1 Timothy 4:1). Many people struggle with tempting, accusing and blasphemous thoughts that reveal a spiritual battle for their minds.

If Satan can convince us to believe a lie, he will keep us in bondage emotionally, mentally and spiritually, and we will lose at least some degree of control over our lives. His primary strategy is to distort the truth about our identity and position in Christ and also our understanding of God. We need to understand what Scripture says about this battle for our minds in order to protect our walk with God.

SATAN THE DECEIVER

Just as God created everything on Earth, He also created the angels in heaven. One of these angels was named Lucifer, which means "light bearer." This angel reflected the light and glory of God. A very beautiful angel, Lucifer was prideful and self-centered, and he challenged the throne of God (see Isaiah 14:12-14). Because of this rebellious act, Lucifer and the angels who had sided with him were cast out of heaven by God.

After the Fall, humankind lost its position and relationship with God, and Satan became the rebel holder of authority over this fallen world. Jesus referred to Satan as "the ruler of this world" (John 12:31). He also called him "the prince of the power of the air" (Ephesians 2:2), and said that the whole world lies in his power (see 1 John 5:19) primarily because he has deceived the inhabitants of the earth (see Revelation 13:14).

THE POSITION OF THE BELIEVER

Authority is the right to rule, and power is the ability to rule. As Christians we have authority over the kingdom of darkness because of our position in Christ. We have the authority to do God's will—nothing more and nothing less. As long as we are controlled by the Holy Spirit, we have the power to do His will. Paul summarized this truth in Ephesians 6:10: "Finally, be strong in the Lord and in the strength of His might."

Satan is a created being and does not have the attributes of God. He is not omnipresent, so his rule over this earth is accomplished through a demonic hierarchy. Jesus came to undo the works of Satan (see 1 John 3:8). He defeated Satan at the Cross and disarmed him (see Colossians 2:15). All authority in heaven *and* on Earth has been given to Jesus because of His crucifixion, resurrection and ascension. Jesus commissioned His disciples to go into all the world and make other disciples (see Matthew 28:18-19). Because of the finished work of Christ, the Church is given the power and authority to continue the work of Christ. Never forget that Christians live victoriously *only* when we rely on God's resources and live in His power.

Even though he is defeated, Satan still "prowls around like a roaring lion, seeking someone to devour" (1 Peter 5:8). We are admonished by Paul to put on the armor of God and stand firm (see Ephesians 6:11). There is *no* time when it is safe to take off the armor of God. Our only sanctuary is our position in Christ!

Ask volunteers to read the following ways in which we are identified in Christ (participants also have the list on page 38 in their student guide) and their corresponding verses.

We Are Identified with Christ

In His death	Romans 6:3; Galatians 2:20; Colossians 3:1-3
In His burial	Romans 6:4
In His resurrection	Romans 6:5,8,11
In His ascension	Ephesians 2:6
In His life	Romans 5:10
In His power	Ephesians 1:19-20
In His inheritance	Romans 8:16-17; Ephesians 1:11-12

THE BATTLE FOR OUR MINDS

In Ephesians 6:11-17, Paul used the metaphor of armor in describing our spiritual protection because armor stops penetration. The "belt of truth" (*NIV*) stands against the devil's deception. The "breastplate of righteousness" stands against Satan's accusations. Putting up the "shield of faith" stands against Satan's assault on our minds, which is where the primary battle is waged. Satan first tempts us to live independently of God, and then when we sin, he becomes the accuser. Every Christian has experienced his temptations and accusations, but the real struggle is deception. That is why truth sets us free.

Share the high priestly prayer that Jesus prayed for all those who believed in Him:

> I have given them Your Word; and the world has hated them, because they are not of the world, even as I am not of the world. I do not ask You to take them out of the world, but to keep them from the evil one. They are not of the world, even as I am not of the world. Sanctify them in the truth; Your word is truth. As You sent Me into the world, I also have sent them into the world (John 17:14-18).

Pause for Thought
Why must you trust the Word of God concerning the spiritual world, which you cannot detect with your five natural senses?

The Example of David

Even David, a man wholly devoted to God, experienced deception when "Satan stood up against Israel and moved David to number Israel" (1 Chronicles 21:1). David was deceived by Satan into thinking what he was doing was his idea—but Scripture tells us that it was Satan who put the thought into David's head. Good people can be deceived, and the fact that the enemy can put thoughts in our minds in such a way that we think they are our own thoughts is what makes the battle so difficult.

The Teaching of Paul

Paul voiced his concern for believers in 2 Corinthians 2:10-11; 4:3-4; 11:3 and 1 Timothy 4:1 when he wrote "I am afraid that, as the serpent deceived Eve by his craftiness, your minds will be led astray from the simplicity and purity of devotion to Christ . . . the Spirit explicitly says that in later times some will fall away

from the faith, paying attention to deceitful spirits and doctrines of demons." This is presently happening all over the world.

Pause for Thought
How can you stand up against deception if you don't know you are being deceived?

Renewing the Mind

The Bible teaches that we are to use our minds actively and not passively. We should focus our thoughts externally, not internally. The most dangerous thing we can do spiritually is to assume a passive state of mind. God never bypasses our minds—He works through them. It is appropriate to invite the Lord to examine our hearts and minds. "Search me, O God, and know my heart; try me and know my anxious thoughts; and see if there be any hurtful way in me" (Psalm 139:23-24).

Pause for Thought
Paul wrote, "The god of this world has blinded the minds [noema] of the unbelieving so that they might not see the light of the gospel of the glory of Christ" (2 Corinthians 4:4). What implications might this have on world evangelization?

If there is a spiritual battle going on for our minds, why aren't we aware of it? Satan and his demons are spiritual beings. They do not have material substance, so we cannot see or hear them with our natural eyes and ears. "For our struggle is not against flesh and blood, but against the rulers, against the powers, against the world forces of this darkness, against the spiritual forces of wickedness in the heavenly places" (Ephesians 6:12). The battle is in the mind. Repentance and faith in God has been and will continue to be the answer. We do this by submitting to God and resisting the devil (see James 4:7). Don't assume that all disturbing thoughts are from Satan, however. Whether the thoughts come from the television set, from our memory bank, from the pit of hell or from our own imagination doesn't matter in one sense because the answer is the same: We must examine every thought, and then choose to believe and think only that which is true.

Suppose we want to clean up our minds. When we make that decision, does the battle get easier or harder? It gets harder, of course. Temptation isn't much of a battle if we easily give in to it. It is fierce when we decide to stand against it. We all have had negative images, immoral pictures and lying thoughts in our minds. How do we get them out? The truth is that we can't—but we can still experience victory.

Share the following illustration:

> Imagine that your mind is like a coffeepot filled with coffee. What you really desire is for the pot to have nothing but clear, clean water. The problem is that there's no place to empty the pot. Sitting beside the coffeepot is a huge bowl of crystal clear ice, which represents the Word of God. Because you are only able to add one or two cubes of ice per day, the process of clearing up the water may seem a little futile at first. If you continue to add ice each day, however, you will begin to see the color of the water turning a lighter color as the coffee becomes more diluted. As long as you continue the process, the contents of the coffeepot will become more like water and less like coffee—provided, of course, that you don't add more coffee.

Winning the battle for our minds will initially be two steps forward and one step back. As we continue, our progress will become three steps forward and one back, then four and five steps forward as we learn to take every thought captive in obedience to Christ. Remember that even though there will be steps backward, God isn't going to give up on us; our sins are already forgiven. The bigger battle has already been won by Christ, and the key to our success is to continue living by faith and keep choosing to believe the truth.

The freedom to be all God has called us to be is the greatest blessing in this present life. This freedom is worth fighting for. As we learn more about who we are as children of God and the nature of the battle that is going on for our minds, the process gets easier. Eventually it will be 20 steps forward and 1 back, and finally the steps are all forward with only an occasional slip in the battle for the mind.

"Let the peace of Christ rule in your hearts, to which indeed you were called in one body: and be thankful" (Colossians 3:15). How do we accomplish this? "Let the word of Christ richly dwell within you" (Colossians 3:16). We must fill our minds with the crystal clear Word of God—there is no alternative plan. If we simply try to stop thinking bad thoughts and rebuke tempting, accusing and deceiving thoughts, we are like a person in the middle of a lake who is trying to keep 12 corks submerged with a small hammer while treading water. We will never make any progress because the corks will continue to pop back up. So what should we do? Ignore the corks and swim to shore, under God's protection! We are not called to dispel the darkness—we are called to turn on the light. We overcome the father of lies by choosing the truth.

> How can a young man keep his way pure? By keeping it according to Your word. With all my heart I have sought You; do not let me wander from Your commandments. Your word I have treasured in my heart, that I might not sin against You (Psalm 119:9-11).

There is a peace of God, which surpasses all comprehension, that will guard your hearts and your minds (noema) in Christ Jesus (see Philippians 4:7).

> Finally, brethren, whatever is true, whatever is honorable, whatever is right, whatever is pure, whatever is lovely, whatever is of good repute, if there is any excellence and if anything worthy of praise, dwell on these things. The things you have learned and received and heard and seen in me, practice these things, and the God of peace will be with you (Philippians 4:8-9).

Explain to participants that unresolved conflict keeps Christians treading water, and that it is only through experiencing freedom in Christ that we can swim to shore. In the last session of this course, participants will be given the opportunity to resolve their personal and spiritual conflicts so that they may experience freedom in Christ.

WITNESS

The following question will help participants begin to formulate ideas for sharing their faith with others. Ask volunteers to offer suggestions for witnessing to nonbelievers, and encourage participants to write down ideas in their student guide.

Freeing people from demonic strongholds was the primary appeal of the gospel in the Early Church and the basis for much of the Early Church's evangelistic efforts. Since Satan has blinded the minds of your non-Christian friends, how can you be a positive witness to them?

GROUP DISCUSSION QUESTIONS

Instruct participants to form small groups of four to six, and assign each group several questions to discuss. Allow several minutes for discussion; then bring the whole group back together, and have volunteers from each small group share their group's questions and answers.

1. If Satan has been defeated and disarmed, how is he able to rule this world?

2. If the struggle in your mind can consist of mental strongholds, or flesh patterns, or it can be a spiritual battle for your mind, how can you tell the difference?

   Do you need to know the difference? Why?

3. What is the difference between power and authority?

   Which do believers have in the spiritual realm, and what qualifies them to have either?

4. Read Ephesians 6:10-18. Putting on the armor of God requires an action by the believer. What must you do to actively put on the armor of God?

   What has Christ already done that we no longer have to do?

5. What is the practical difference between trying not to think negative thoughts and choosing to think upon that which is true?

6. How can you renew your mind?

7. How can you stop treading water and instead swim to shore?

TAKING IT WITH YOU

The following information is included in the student guide and is intended for participants to use during the upcoming week. Direct participants to this section and encourage them to do the quiet-time suggestion and to consider the Big Question before your next session.

SUGGESTION FOR QUIET TIME

Meditate every day during the coming week on each of the following verses:
- Matthew 28:18
- Ephesians 1:3-14; 2:6-10
- Colossians 2:13-15

THE BIG QUESTION

Before the next session, consider the following question:

If we can't always believe what we feel, how should we deal with our emotions?

EMOTIONAL FREEDOM

THEREFORE, LAYING ASIDE FALSEHOOD, SPEAK TRUTH EACH ONE OF
YOU WITH HIS NEIGHBOR, FOR WE ARE MEMBERS OF ONE ANOTHER.
BE ANGRY, AND YET DO NOT SIN; DO NOT LET THE SUN GO DOWN
ON YOUR ANGER, AND DO NOT GIVE THE DEVIL AN OPPORTUNITY.
EPHESIANS 4:25-27

CASTING ALL YOUR ANXIETY ON HIM, BECAUSE HE CARES FOR YOU.
BE OF SOBER SPIRIT, BE ON THE ALERT. YOUR ADVERSARY, THE DEVIL,
PROWLS AROUND LIKE A ROARING LION, SEEKING SOMEONE TO DEVOUR.
1 PETER 5:7-8

SESSION OVERVIEW

OBJECTIVE

In this session, you will help participants understand what the emotional nature is, how our emotions affect what we believe and how we can be emotionally free from the past.

FOCUS TRUTH

Our emotions are essentially a product of our thoughts and beliefs, and they can be an effective barometer of our spiritual health.

BRIEFING

When God created human beings, He equipped us with a complex emotional nature. Thus far in this course you have challenged participants to believe that what God says is true regardless of their feelings. This is different from denying their feelings, however, and it is important to understand that emotions are directly affected by what they believe and how they live their lives. The information in this session will provide a critical link in preparation for the emotional healing that participants will experience when they go through the Steps to Freedom in Christ later in this course.

Note:
For additional information on resolving specific emotional problems, we recommend the following resources:
• Neil T. Anderson and Rich Miller, Getting Anger Under Control (Harvest House, 2002) for information on **resolving anger**
• Neil T. Anderson and Rich Miller, Freedom from Fear (Harvest House, 1999) for information on **resolving anxiety disorders**
• Neil T. Anderson, Overcoming Depression (Regal Books, 2004) for information on **resolving depression**

EMOTIONAL FREEDOM

THEREFORE, LAYING ASIDE FALSEHOOD, SPEAK TRUTH EACH ONE OF
YOU WITH HIS NEIGHBOR, FOR WE ARE MEMBERS OF ONE ANOTHER.
BE ANGRY, AND YET DO NOT SIN; DO NOT LET THE SUN GO DOWN
ON YOUR ANGER, AND DO NOT GIVE THE DEVIL AN OPPORTUNITY.
EPHESIANS 4:25-27

CASTING ALL YOUR ANXIETY ON HIM, BECAUSE HE CARES FOR YOU.
BE OF SOBER SPIRIT, BE ON THE ALERT. YOUR ADVERSARY, THE DEVIL,
PROWLS AROUND LIKE A ROARING LION, SEEKING SOMEONE TO DEVOUR.
1 PETER 5:7-8

WELCOME

Welcome participants and invite a volunteer to open the meeting in prayer; then share the following story:

As the Father welcomed His newly adopted child into His home, He said, "This is yours and you have a right to be here. I have made you a joint heir with My only begotten Son. He paid the price so that you could be set free from your old taskmaster, who was cruel and condemning. I did this because I love you."

Although he had no idea what he could have done to deserve such a privilege, the boy was deeply grateful and began to explore all the rooms in the mansion. As he explored, he found that he had many brothers and sisters who had also been adopted. He especially enjoyed the buffet table from which he freely ate. One day while turning from the buffet table, the young boy accidentally bumped against a stack of glasses and a valuable pitcher, and all went crashing to the floor. Terrified, the boy thought, *I'm so clumsy and stupid! I'm going to be in so much trouble—I'd better find somewhere to hide before someone finds out what I did!*

Although he had been told by his Father that he was loved, the boy was filled with guilt and shame as thoughts kept coming. *The old taskmaster was right about me—I'm not good enough to be here.* Ashamed, the boy hid in the dreary, dark and despairing cellar. The only light came from the open door at the top of the long stairs from which he had descended. He heard his Father calling for him, but he was too afraid to answer back. Once his eyes adjusted to the darkness, the boy found he was not alone in the cellar. Unlike the children upstairs, no one in the cellar talked to each other. Each stared longingly at the light at the top of the stairs, but few ventured out of the cellar. Some were too ashamed to climb the stairs and others were fearful that they would not make it to the top. Some would go up for a short time only to return because they couldn't resolve their conflicts and learn the truth that would enable them to stay.

The longer the boy stayed in the cellar, the dimmer his memory of his life upstairs became. He began to remember all the horrible things the taskmaster had done and said to him, and so he also began to question whether he had ever been adopted in the first place. Soon, the noise of people having fun upstairs irritated him. The light from upstairs that had once seemed warm and inviting was now penetrating and revealing. He tried hard to recall something he had heard his adoptive Father say: "Men loved the darkness rather than the Light, for their deeds were evil. For everyone who does evil hates the Light, and does not come to the Light for fear that his deeds will be exposed" (John 3:19-20).

One day a shaft of light penetrated his mind and reason returned. He began to think, *Why not throw myself on the mercy of this person who calls Himself my Father. What do I have to lose? Even if He makes me eat the crumbs that fall from the table to the floor, it would be better than this.* So the boy resolved to go upstairs and face his Father with the truth of what he had done that day at the buffet. "Father," he began while he cried, "I knocked over some glasses and broke a pitcher." Without saying a word, his Father took him by the hand and led him into the dining room. Shaking with fear, the boy was sure the Father was about to punish him in front of everyone, just as his taskmaster had done so many times. To his utter amazement, the Father had prepared a banquet—in his honor. "Welcome home," his Father said. Then his Father said the most wonderful thing: "There is now no condemnation for those who are in Christ Jesus" (Romans 8:1).

Briefly discuss the following questions to help participants practically apply the parable about the adopted boy to real-life situations:

1. Do you know of any Christians who are emotionally stuck in the cellar like the boy in the story? (**Note:** Be sure participants don't use this question as an opening to gossip about anyone. Encourage those who share not to use actual names in their answer.)

2. What kinds of things make you react like the boy and run away and hide from your heavenly Father?

What can you do to avoid having this reaction?

WORSHIP

Spend a few minutes worshiping the Lord through prayer, song, praise or testimonies shared by volunteers.

WORD

 The Word section is available on the Beta DVD, or you can present the information yourself in a lecture format.

EMOTIONAL FREEDOM

Share the following case study:

Judy was a 26-year-old university graduate with a teaching credential. When she first went to see her pastor for counseling, she looked like a flower child from the '60s. She wore tattered jeans, had on no shoes and carried a Bible stained with tears with her everywhere she went. Judy had been institutionalized three times in the previous five years and was classified as a paranoid schizophrenic, because of her many fears and the voices in her head.

She began to meet on a weekly basis with her pastor. When he asked her to come under the authority of their church, her countenance changed and she had to get out of there. The pastor had enough discernment to sense the spiritual opposition, but he lacked the experience to deal with it. Knowing that she was in spiritual bondage, he assumed she must be living an immoral life or involved in the occult, but neither was the case. The pastor was able to ascertain that her problems began when her father left her mother and married his lover. Whenever the pastor brought up the subject, she wanted to leave the room. She couldn't seem to handle anything emotionally troubling to her.

Judy's pastor started to see the spiritual connection with her emotional difficulties when he discovered two passages of Scripture. The first was Ephesians 4:25-27: "Therefore, laying aside falsehood, speak truth each one of you with his neighbor, for we are members of one another. Be angry, and yet do not sin; do not let the sun go down on your anger, and do not give the devil an opportunity." Judy's unresolved anger toward her father was never confessed; and since she had repressed her anger instead of dealing with it, she had given the devil an opportunity, a foothold, literally a place in her life.

The second passage was 1 Peter 5:7-8: "Casting all your anxiety on Him, because He cares for you. Be of sober spirit, be on the alert. Your adversary, the devil, prowls around like a roaring lion, seeking someone to devour." Instead of casting her anxieties about her father upon the Lord, Judy thought she was being spiritual by covering them up. Judy's emotional dishonesty left her spiritually vulnerable.

Judy began to face her unresolved feelings toward her father and work through the issue of forgiveness, which was the crux of her problem. This young woman made significant progress and became involved in the ministry of her church.

OUR EMOTIONS REVEAL WHAT WE THINK AND BELIEVE

In a general sense, our emotions are a product of our thought life. If we are not thinking right and our minds are not being renewed—if we are not correctly believing God and His Word—it will show up in our emotional life. If we fail to appropriately acknowledge our emotions, we may become spiritually vulnerable, as the previous story illustrates.

For a scriptural illustration of the connection between beliefs and emotions, consider Lamentations 3. Jeremiah expressed despair when he (wrongly) perceived that God was against him and that God was the cause of his problems. Read verses 1 through 6 aloud.

In verses 7 through 11 and verse 18, Jeremiah wrote about his feelings of entrapment and fear. Invite a volunteer to read these verses.

What Jeremiah believed about God wasn't true; God wasn't the cause of his affliction. God didn't make him walk in darkness. God wasn't a wild beast waiting to devour him. Jeremiah wasn't thinking or interpreting his circumstances correctly, and so he wasn't feeling or living right as a result.

In verses 19 through 24, we can see how Jeremiah began to think differently. Have another volunteer read these verses aloud.

Did God Himself change? Did Jeremiah's circumstances change? No and no. What brought about this change? The change was in Jeremiah's thinking. When Jeremiah's thoughts about God changed, his emotions did too. The Bible admonishes us to believe God and His Word, live accordingly by faith and let our emotions be a product of our trust in God and our obedience to Him.

Pause for Thought
How might your life be different if you believed what you felt even though what you felt conflicted with the truth?

If we believed in our feelings even when our feelings conflicted with the truth, our lives would be as inconsistent as our feelings. After the Fall, God said to Cain, "Why are you angry? And why has your countenance fallen? If you do well, will not your countenance be lifted up?" (Genesis 4:6-7). Jesus said to His disciples, "If you know these things, you are blessed if you do them" (John 13:17). In other words, we don't feel our way into good behavior; we behave our way into good feelings.

WAYS WE RESPOND TO OUR EMOTIONS

Emotions are to our souls what physical feeling is to our bodies. God gave us the ability to feel physical pain for our protection—if we didn't feel pain, we wouldn't know when we were physically hurt! Our emotions are much like an indicator light on the instrument panel of a car. When the light turns red, we know something is not right with the car. It could be something as simple as a reminder that we're almost out of gas, or it could be indicating that our engine is too hot. Whatever the problem, the red light serves as a warning to us.

When the red light goes on, there are three basic ways in which we can respond:

1. Cover it up. *I can't see it, so there must not be a problem.* This is called suppression.
2. Smash it. *That stupid warning light won't be bothering* me *again!* This is called indiscriminate expression.
3. Look under the hood. *I'd better see what's causing the warning and fix the problem.* This is called acknowledgment.

Suppression

Unlike repression, which is an unconscious denial of feelings, those of us who suppress our emotions make a conscious choice to ignore them. Suppression is physically unhealthy, and it is also dishonest. Consider how King David felt when he lived in denial:

When I kept silent about my sin, my body wasted away through my groaning all day long. Therefore, let everyone who is godly pray to You in a time when You may be found; surely in a flood of great waters they will not reach him (Psalm 32:3,6).

David was not saying that God is unreachable. Instead, he was pointing out that when we allow our circumstances to loom larger than God, we become emotionally overwhelmed. When suppressed emotions build up within us like "great waters," we will be driven by our emotions and less likely to turn to God. It is important to be honest with God and not bottle up our feelings so that we can keep them from dominating our lives. David recognized the importance of this in Psalm 39:

> I said, "I will guard my ways that I may not sin with my tongue; I will guard my mouth as with a muzzle while the wicked are in my presence." I was mute and silent, I refrained even from good, and my sorrow grew worse (vv. 1-2).

Notice that David said his sorrow "grew worse." He recognized that denial does not work! He also saw that when he kept quiet about his sins his "vitality was drained away as with the fever heat of summer" (Psalm 32:4). Feelings don't die when we bury them; they are buried alive, leading to dishonest communication and surfacing in unhealthy ways.

Indiscriminate Expression

Another unhealthy way to respond to our emotions is thoughtless expression of everything we feel. Instead of bottling up our feelings, we constantly blurt out how we feel without regard to those around us. This can cause major damage to our relationships with others.

> But everyone must be quick to hear, slow to speak and slow to anger; for the anger of man does not achieve the righteousness of God" (James 1:19-20).
>
> Be angry, and yet do not sin (Ephesians 4:26).

If we wish to be angry and not sin, then we should look to Jesus' example and be angry *at* sin. Remember how He turned over the tables—not the money changers (see Matthew 21:12).

Acknowledgment

Acknowledging how we feel and then working to resolve the underlying problem is the key to dealing with our emotions in a healthy way. Emotional honesty begins with God. Read Psalm 109:1-13 aloud, or ask a volunteer to read it.

David's words didn't surprise God—God already knew what he was thinking and feeling. God wanted David to express his pain and anger honestly to Him, which inspired David to write down how he felt. We can't be right with God and not be real, and there are times when God may have to make us real in order for us to be right with Him.

RESPONDING TO EMOTIONAL HONESTY FROM OTHERS

One of the great challenges in life is learning how to respond to others when they acknowledge their pain. It can be difficult to learn that we should respond to the pain, not the words used to express it. Too often we fixate on what someone says or how he or she says it instead of concentrating on the pain behind the words. Job knew this and admonished his friends (who had been less than helpful) by asking, "Do you intend to reprove my words, when the words of one in despair belong to the wind?" (Job 6:26).

In John 11, when grief-stricken sisters Mary and Martha both met Jesus and said, "Lord, if You had been here, my brother would not have died" (vv. 21,32), He did not respond to their words but to the pain behind them. Verse 35 tells us that not only did Jesus respond to their pain but also that He cried openly with them.

"Rejoice with those who rejoice, and weep with those who weep" (Romans 12:15). We are not supposed to *instruct* those who weep; we are to show compassion and empathy toward them. For example, say a Christian couple you know loses an infant to sudden infant death syndrome (SIDS). Overcome with grief, each asks you why God would allow such a thing to happen. You will probably be tempted to give some theological explanation, but in reality you don't know why God allowed this tragedy to happen. Their words reveal the intensity of their pain, and the proper response from you is empathy. There will be ample time later for appropriate theological answers, if that is possible and necessary, after the emotional pain of their tragic loss has subsided.

Sharing Emotional Honesty in Relationships

Learning to speak the truth in love includes emotional honesty. To illustrate this, let's take a look at a couple we'll call Gary and Dawn:

Gary was having a terrible day at the office and called home to let his wife, Dawn, know he would be late coming home that evening, and he asked if she could be sure to have dinner ready because he would have less than an hour to make it to the 7:00 P.M. church meeting by the time he got home.

When Gary came through the front door, he was physically exhausted and emotionally wiped out. Upon discovering that dinner was not ready, Gary confronted Dawn. "For crying out loud, why isn't dinner ready? That's why I called you this afternoon; I don't have a lot of time before I have to leave for that meeting!"

Briefly discuss the underlying reasons that caused Gary to explode at Dawn: He had had a bad day; he was tired and hungry; and he had even more work ahead of him that evening at the church meeting. Truthfully, just about anything could have triggered Gary's tantrum. Does this type of behavior qualify as emotional honesty?

Let's take a look at an alternate approach as Gary arrives home:

When Gary came through the front door, he was physically exhausted and emotionally wiped out—ready to explode. Upon discovering that dinner was not ready, he said to his wife, "Honey, I'm near the end of my rope physically and emotionally."

That kind of emotional honesty accomplishes two important things: First, by not blaming his wife for his bad mood, Gary opened the door for her to respond with compassion. She can say something like, "Why don't you go into the den and relax? I'll have the kids help me set the table so that you can relax. Dinner will be ready in about 15 minutes, and then you can get ready for your meeting."

Now let's turn the tables a bit and look at Gary and Dawn on another day:

Dawn was in the middle of a tough day when Gary called. Because it was raining, all three of their young children had been stuck inside all day and were constantly whining to her or fighting with each other. The thought of even cooking dinner was overwhelming, but she was trying to have it done by the time Gary came home.

When Gary walked in the door and nicely asked if dinner was close to being ready so that he would have time to eat before he had to leave again, Dawn exploded. "Is that all you think I have to do during the day? Don't you think I work too? Why don't *you* try acting as a referee to the kids all day, and I'll go get a job?! At least you get out of the house every day!"

While this is a display of emotional honesty, it's not the most productive way to approach it. What if she were to say, "Oh, Gary, I've just had it. The washing machine broke in the middle of my doing laundry, and the kids have been driving me nuts today. I feel like I'm really on the edge right now." That type of expression is an "I" reaction, and not a "you" judgment. This type of emotional honesty allows Gary to spend less energy fending off verbal arrows and more energy helping find an immediate solution to the dinner problem. Pizza anyone?

Knowing Our Emotional Limits

We should be able to gauge our emotional limitations. If we are emotionally exhausted, we should not confront others or make important decisions. Realize also that there are many physical factors that will affect our emotional limits, including hunger and exhaustion. If you're hungry, postpone a potentially emotionally charged discussion until after you've eaten. Likewise, if you're tired, get a good night's sleep. The important process of renewing our minds includes managing our emotions by managing our thoughts and acknowledging our feelings honestly and lovingly in our relationships with others.

HEALING EMOTIONAL WOUNDS FROM THE PAST

Traumatic experiences in our past can leave deep emotional scars. Any number of traumatic events (e.g., physical, emotional, verbal and sexual abuse; a severe scare; death; divorce) can stay buried in our memories and remain available for instant recall.

All of us have been affected emotionally by our past experiences, and those experiences contribute to how we react to any particular subject. For example, someone who has experienced the trauma of rape—either personally or through a close loved one's rape—will have a reaction to the subject of rape different from that of someone whose experience is limited to having read about it or heard about it via the media.

Even something as simple as a name can prompt an emotional response. If your kind, loving grandfather was named Bill, you probably have a favorable emotional reaction to other people named Bill. But if your first boss was a tyrant named Bill, or if the school bully was named Bill, your initial reaction to the other Bills in your life is probably negative. If your spouse suggests, "Let's name our first son Bill," you might respond, "Over my dead body!"

Primary Emotions—The Residual Effect of Past Traumas

The intensity of our primary emotions is determined by our previous life history. The more traumatic the experience, the more intense the primary emotion. Notice the sequence of events:

- **Previous Life History**—determines the intensity of primary emotions
- **Present Event**—triggers the primary emotion
- **Primary Emotion**—displays residual effect of past traumas
- **Mental Evaluation**—manages the emotions
- **Secondary Emotion**—occurs as a result of the thought process and primary emotion

Many primary emotions lie dormant and have a negligible effect on us until they are triggered by a present event. The trigger is any present event that can be associated with past conflicts. For example, let's say John is out to lunch with a colleague when he hears a siren up the street. When John was a small boy, his mother was rushed to the hospital in an ambulance several times. Without consciously connecting the sound of the siren to his next thought, John has the sudden urge to check up on his mom when he gets back to the office.

Most of us try to control our primary emotions by avoiding the people or events that trigger them. "I'm not going if *he's* going to be there." "I can't watch that kind of a movie because it hits too close to home."

"I don't want to talk about that subject." It's unreasonable for us to expect that we can isolate ourselves completely from anything that may trigger an emotional response. Instead, we must recognize that these emotions are rooted in the past and that something in our past is unresolved and therefore still has a hold on us.

Obviously, we have no control over our primary emotions—but we can stabilize a primary emotion by evaluating it in light of present circumstances. For example, suppose our friend John meets a new client named Bill. Bill looks like the schoolyard bully also named Bill who used to pick on John. Even though this Bill is not the same one from John's childhood, John's primary emotion will be triggered. John's responsibility at this point is to evaluate his primary emotion in light of the present circumstance. He reasons with himself: *This isn't the same Bill from the playground, even though he reminds me of him. I need to give this guy the benefit of the doubt.* This quick mental evaluation produces a secondary emotion, which is a combination of the past and the present.

SEEING OUR PAST IN LIGHT OF WHO WE ARE IN CHRIST

Most people have had major traumas in their past. For some people, there have been events so traumatic that they have no conscious memory of them. Others avoid anything that will trigger painful memories. We develop many different defense mechanisms in order to cope with our past, from living in denial to rationalizing our problems to suppressing our pain with food, drugs or sex.

According to Psalm 139:23-24, we can invite the Lord to examine us: "Search me, O God, and know my heart; try me and know my anxious thoughts; and see if there be any hurtful way in me, and lead me in the everlasting way." God knows all about the hidden hurts within us that we may not be aware of. He alone can bind up the broken hearted and set the captives free. When we ask God to search our heart, He will expose those dark areas of our past and bring them to light at the right time. The Holy Spirit "will guide you into all the truth" (John 16:13), and that truth will set us free.

We can't fix our past. God doesn't even do that for us. He does something better: He sets us free from our past! First, when we accepted Christ, we were no longer a product of our past; we became a new creation in Christ (see 2 Corinthians 5:17). We have the awesome privilege of evaluating our past experiences in the light of who we are today, as opposed to who we were then. People are not in bondage to past traumas; they are in bondage to the lies they believed about themselves, God and life as a result of the trauma. That is why truth sets us free (see John 8:31-32), and we can be transformed by the renewing of our minds (see Romans 12:2). Although the flesh patterns will remain embedded in our minds, we can crucify the flesh and choose to walk by the Spirit (Galatians 5:24-25).

The second means by which we experience freedom from our past is through forgiveness. When we hold on to unforgiveness, it is we who are captive. In the next session, we are going to discuss what forgiveness is and what it isn't, and then share how we can forgive from our hearts and appropriate our own freedom that we have in Christ.

Our old nature will seek revenge, but the Spirit of God will set us free. Share the following illustration:

> Once I held in my tightly clenched fist ashes, ashes from a burn that flickered upon my ten-year-old body, ashes I didn't ask for. The scar was forced on me and for seventeen years the fire smoldered. I kept my fist closed in secret, hating those ashes, yet unwilling to release them, not sure if I should, not convinced that it was worth it, marring the things that I touched and leaving black marks everywhere or so it seemed. I tried to undo it all but the ashes were always there to remind me that I couldn't. I really could not, but God could. His sweet Holy Spirit spoke to my heart one night in tearful desperation. He whispered "I want to give you beauty for your ashes, oil of joy for your mourning, a garment of praise for your spirit of heaviness." I had never heard of such a trade as this—beauty for ashes, my sadly stained memory for the healing in His Word, my sootlike dreams for His songs in the night, my helpless and hurting emotions for His ever constant peace. How could I be so stubborn as to refuse an offer such as this? So willingly yet in slow motion and yes sobbing, I opened my bent fingers and let the ashes drop to the ground. In silence, I heard the wind blow them away, away from me forever. I am now able to place

> my open hands gently round the fist of another hurting soul and say with confidence, "Let them go." There really is beauty beyond your comprehension. Go ahead, trust Him. His beauty for your ashes.[1]

WITNESS

The following two questions will help participants begin to formulate ideas for sharing their faith with others. Invite volunteers to offer suggestions for witnessing to nonbelievers, and encourage participants to write down ideas in their student guide.

1. If you are feeling angry, anxious or depressed, do you think it would be better not to be emotionally honest in the presence of non-Christians?

2. Would that be an effective or ineffective witness for Christ? Why?

GROUP DISCUSSION QUESTIONS

Instruct participants to form small groups of four to six, and assign each group several questions to discuss. Allow several minutes for discussion; then bring the whole group back together, and have volunteers from each small group share their group's questions and answers.

1. In what way could emotional dishonesty give the devil a foothold in your life?

2. What did you experience more in your home while growing up: emotional denial or indiscriminate expression? How has that affected your life?

3. In what ways can emotional dishonesty precipitate psychosomatic illnesses (i.e., physical illnesses whose root cause is emotional or mental in nature)?

4. How should you respond when someone who is hurting emotionally becomes verbally abusive?

5. How can you learn to recognize your emotional limitations?

6. What happens when something or someone triggers a strong emotion in you? What is your first reaction?

7. How can we become emotionally free from our past?

TAKING IT WITH YOU

The following information is included in the student guide and is intended for participants to use during the upcoming week. Direct participants to this section and encourage them to do the quiet-time suggestions and to consider the Big Question before the next session.

SUGGESTIONS FOR QUIET TIME

Consider the emotional nature of the apostle Peter. First, look at some occasions when he acted impulsively or spoke too hastily:

- Matthew 16:21-23
- Matthew 17:1-5
- John 18:1-11

Now read Matthew 16:17-19 to see how Jesus looked beyond Peter's emotional outbursts to see Peter's potential, and finally, read Acts 2:14-41 to see how—under the power of the Holy Spirit—Peter fulfilled his potential and became the spokesperson of the Early Church.

THE BIG QUESTION

Before the next session, consider the following question:

How do you forgive from your heart those who have offended or deeply wounded you?

Note
1. Neil T. Anderson and Hal Baumchen, *Finding Hope Again* (Ventura, CA: Regal Books, 1999) pp. 159-161.

FORGIVING FROM THE HEART

LET ALL BITTERNESS AND WRATH AND ANGER AND CLAMOR AND SLANDER BE PUT AWAY
FROM YOU, ALONG WITH ALL MALICE. BE KIND TO ONE ANOTHER, TENDER-HEARTED,
FORGIVING EACH OTHER, JUST AS GOD IN CHRIST ALSO HAS FORGIVEN YOU.
EPHESIANS 4:31-32

SESSION OVERVIEW

OBJECTIVE

In this session you will help participants understand the nature of forgiveness and learn how to forgive from the heart as Christ has forgiven them.

FOCUS TRUTH

In order to experience our freedom in Christ, we must relate to other people in the same way God relates to us.

BRIEFING

Forgiveness is the central issue in Christianity, and forgiving from the heart is the most important decision we can make in order to experience our freedom in Christ. Most Christians know they should forgive, but few fully understand what forgiveness is and how to forgive others from the heart. Some are reluctant to forgive because to do so would mean letting go of the desire to seek revenge; others hold on to anger and unforgiveness with the false expectation that this will protect them in the future. Forgiveness begins with God, and the love, mercy and grace that we have received from God we are to extend to others.

FORGIVING FROM THE HEART

Let all bitterness and wrath and anger and clamor and slander be put away from you, along with all malice. Be kind to one another, tender-hearted, forgiving each other, just as God in Christ also has forgiven you.
Ephesians 4:31-32

WELCOME

Welcome participants and show them a $20 bill. Ask how many would like to have it. Then wad it up and ask, "Now how many would like to have this $20 bill?" Put the money on the floor and step on it; then ask the same question again. Explain that many of us have been crumpled and stepped on by many adversities in life but that our value remains the same—just like the $20 bill.

Ask for five volunteers to read Matthew 18:21-35 aloud, each reading three verses. After the reading, facilitate a brief group discussion regarding which particular parts of the parable impacted people the most and why.

WORSHIP

Spend a few minutes worshiping the Lord through prayer, song, praise or testimonies shared by volunteers.

WORD

 The Word section is available on the Beta DVD, or you can present the information yourself in a lecture format.

Share the following illustration:

There was a woman whose husband had left her for another woman—her best friend.

During the 10 years since this had happened, the woman still held on to her bitterness and anger toward the happy couple. She resented that the couple appeared to be getting on with their life together very well, living in a nice house and taking expensive vacations while she struggled to make ends meet. To top it off, neither her ex-husband or ex-friend showed any remorse for what they had done, or made any attempt at asking her for forgiveness.

One Sunday after listening to the message on forgiveness, the woman approached the pastor and exclaimed, "Forgive them?! You want me to just forgive those two for ruining my life?"

The pastor quietly replied, "I see a hurting person with one arm thrust in the air with a closed fist, but the strong arm of God has a firm grasp around your wrist. Although your hand is not hanging on to God, He is hanging on to you. Your other arm is dragging you down because you are holding on to the past. Why don't you consider letting go of the weight of the past and instead grab hold of God with all your might?"

The woman was sure the pastor didn't understand the depth of her pain. "But you don't understand how badly they hurt me," she protested.

"What I understand is that they are still hurting you," the pastor answered, "and forgiveness is God's way of stopping the pain. When you let go of the past, it no longer has a hold on you and you can reestablish communion with your heavenly Father who loves you. It is not easy to let go of our pain—and that's why it cannot be done without the help of Jesus Christ."

OUR NEED TO EXTEND *AND* RECEIVE FORGIVENESS

Before we can understand what forgiveness is and how to forgive from the heart, we must first understand the distinction between forgiving those who have offended or hurt us and seeking forgiveness from God and others.

Share Matthew 5:23-24:

> If you are presenting your offering at the altar, and there remember that your brother has something against you, leave your offering there before the altar and go; first be reconciled to your brother, and then come and present your offering.

If we have sinned against another person, we must not act as though we have done nothing wrong when the Holy Spirit is convicting us otherwise. We should go to that person with a repentant heart, seek his or her forgiveness and offer to make reparations.

Just as we cannot be right with God if we don't seek forgiveness for offending or hurting others, so we must extend forgiveness to those who have wronged us before we can be right with God. "Forgive us our debts, as we also have forgiven our debtors" (Matthew 6:12). Unlike seeking forgiveness, extending forgiveness is not primarily a matter between us and those who've wronged us. Forgiving others is primarily an issue between us and God, and it is to Him that we are to turn.

What if offenders never ask for our forgiveness? What if they go to their grave without every admitting any wrong? What if we need to extend forgiveness to someone who might hurt us again (e.g., someone who physically hurt us) if we were to personally approach him or her? Does that give us the right to remain bitter and to refuse to forgive that person? Our relationship with God and our freedom in Christ cannot be dependent on other people, because we have no right or ability to control anyone but ourselves.

Pause for Thought

How is reconciliation different from forgiveness? Whose participation is required for forgiveness? Whose participation is required for reconciliation?

THE NEED TO FORGIVE

The need to forgive others was taught by Jesus in Matthew 18:21-35 in response to Peter's question, "Lord, how often shall my brother sin against me and I forgive him? Up to seven times?" (v. 21). Jesus answered, "up to seventy times seven" (v. 22). Jesus was not suggesting that we keep a pocket calculator and tick off 490 times before we explode—He was saying that forgiveness doesn't keep count because continued forgiveness is part of the Christian lifestyle. To illustrate this, He told the parable about the man who owed his master ten thousand talents—more than a lifetime's wages.

Ask a volunteer to read Matthew 18:23-27.

There was no way the man could pay his master, and he had to beg for his master's mercy. In order to make sense of this parable, we need to define three terms: "justice," "mercy" and "grace."

Justice is rightness or fairness; it is giving someone what he or she deserves. Because God is just, He had no choice but to give Adam and Eve what they deserved for their disobedience in the Garden of Eden. The consequence of sin is spiritual death, an eternity apart from God. And because we sin, that is also what we deserve—thankfully God is merciful and sent Jesus to pay the price for our sins. God provided His own Son to pay for our sins with His very life. *Mercy* is not giving us what we deserve.

Not only was God merciful to us in providing Jesus for our salvation, He also continually shows us *grace* by giving us that which we do not deserve. He continues to give us His blessings each day, even though we fall far short of deserving them! In the same way, we are called as followers of Jesus Christ to relate to others in the same way that God relates to us. Not only are we not to give people what they deserve, but we are also to be gracious and give what they need. We are to "love one another" as Jesus has loved us (John 13:34).

Ask a volunteer to read Matthew 18:28-30. The man who had been shown mercy by his master was obviously grateful but failed to show mercy and grace to a fellow slave who owed him money, even though what he was owed—a day's wages—was far less than what he had owed his master. The price Jesus paid for our sins is *far* greater than any price we will ever pay in order to forgive others. We can begin to think that our need for forgiveness is not very great, since there are other people who really do need to be forgiven! This is dangerous thinking, however, because we must never forget that we are all in desperate need of God's mercy and grace.

Every morning, our first thoughts should be of praise and thanksgiving to God for His grace and mercy, professing our knowledge that although we deserve eternal damnation, He has given us eternal life. We should commit ourselves to being who He created us to be and ask for His Holy Spirit to fill our hearts, enabling us to love, accept and forgive others in the same way He has loved, accepted and forgiven us.

Ask a volunteer to read Matthew 18:31-35. The message is clear: We are to forgive others as we have been forgiven. When we fail to do this, we allow ourselves to become trapped in bitterness. We are in bondage to it, unable to free our thoughts from our torment. God doesn't want us to live in the bondage of bitterness, so He disciplines us. We should forgive others from our hearts and thus find the freedom of forgiveness.

Pause for Thought
What would the spiritual consequences be if members of your family and church refused to forgive? Can you experience God's blessings if you remain in bondage to your bitterness?

WHAT FORGIVENESS IS NOT

It is important to understand what forgiveness is *not* in order to fully understand what forgiveness *is*.

It Is Not Forgetting

God doesn't forget our sins—because an omniscient God couldn't forget even if He wanted to—but He has promised that He will not take our past offenses and use them against us in the future. He will remove them from us "as far as the east is from the west" (Psalm 103:12).

Forgiving others doesn't mean that we won't testify later for the purpose of seeking justice or for the purpose of confronting others when we carry out church discipline. We forgive from our hearts in order to be right with God and to be free from the bondage of bitterness. Only then can we properly approach an offending party for the sake of justice without bitterly seeking revenge.

It Is Not Tolerating Sin

Jesus forgives, but He doesn't tolerate sin and neither should we. Shelters for battered women and abused children don't always get the support from the local church they should. One reason for this lack of support is that some of those women and children come from the homes of Christian leaders in those churches. Another reason is the poor advice those victims have received from spiritual leaders in their churches: "Just go home, be submissive and trust God." The Bible does teach that women and children are to be submissive to their husbands and fathers (see Ephesians 5:22-24; 6:1-2), but that is not all the Bible teaches. It also teaches that there are governing authorities who have established laws to protect battered women and abused children (see 1 Peter 2:13-14).

Suppose a complete stranger beats up a woman who is a member in your church. What might be the reaction of the church? Anger? Outrage? But it's okay for a husband to beat up his own wife? If a woman is abusing children in your church's nursery, would you tolerate that? But it's okay to abuse her own children simply because they are her children? It is not only wrong, it is doubly wrong, because God charges the husband to provide for and protect his wife and children, and the mother is to do likewise for her children. So when victims are abused by those who have been charged to protect them, the victims suffer double loss. In addition to being victimized, they no longer have anyone to protect them.

We should report abusers to the proper authorities. Not because we are mean spirited or because we want revenge—rather, we do it because we will never help abusers by allowing them to continue in their abuse. The shelter should teach these victims to forgive their husbands and fathers for the victims' sake—and then teach them how to set up scriptural boundaries to stop further abuse. That is the only way to stop the cycle of abuse and to ensure that the abuser will no longer be allowed to harm others. Abusive people need help, and many won't seek it unless they are confronted and held responsible. We don't seek revenge, but we do seek justice.

A married woman with children said, "I know who I need to forgive—my mother. But if I forgive her tonight, I know what will happen next Sunday. She will come over to our house and bad-mouth me all over again." Without question, this woman should put a stop to this verbal abuse. It will not honor her mother to allow her to systematically destroy her marriage and family. The commandment to honor our parents probably is best understood as instruction for adult children to financially take care of their aging parents. That doesn't mean that younger children shouldn't obey their parents, but this young mother is no longer under the authority of her parents. She should confront her mother about her abuse by saying something like this:

> Mother, I want you to know that I love you and I am thankful for all you have done for me, but I cannot put up with your verbal abuse anymore. It isn't doing you any good, and it certainly isn't doing me any good. If you continue doing it, I am going to insist that you stay away until you learn to respect me and my family. This cycle of abuse is going to stop right here. I have worked through my own bitterness and resentment, and I will not allow this problem to interfere with my responsibility to be a good wife and mother.

Pause for Thought
What happens to forgiveness if you tolerate sin and fail to set scriptural boundaries?

It Is Not Denying Our Pain
Forgiveness is not stuffing our emotions or denying our pain. If we are going to forgive from our hearts, we have to do so from our hearts, and that means acknowledging the hurt and the hate we feel. Someone may say, "I forgave my father for the things he did to me." A friend might reply, "That's terrific. What did you forgive him for?" only to be told "I don't want to talk about it!" This person hasn't forgiven; he or she has simply tried—unsuccessfully—to forget his or her pain.

We must allow God to bring our past to the surface so that we can let it go. If we try to bury our pain, we bury it alive, and it will surface in physical illnesses, emotional problems and interpersonal conflicts. This is generic forgiveness, and if we forgive generically, we get generic freedom in return.

One young lady said, "I can't forgive my mother; I hate her!" The wise pastoral counselor said, "Now you can." God isn't asking us to deny our feelings. Such hypocrisy is inconsistent with the nature of God.

Remember, we can't be right with God and not be real. "Humble yourselves in the presence of the Lord, and He will exalt you" (James 4:10). Millions of Christians have come to terms with their pain and have experienced the blessing of Matthew 5:4: "Blessed are those who mourn, for they shall be comforted." If we have truly forgiven others, we are free from them. To forgive is to set a captive free and then realize that it was us who were captive. That is one reason why moving away from an offender doesn't solve the problem or give us any mental peace. That is just running away from our responsibility to forgive.

WHAT FORGIVENESS *IS*
Concerning how we ought to live with one another, Paul wrote, "Let all bitterness and wrath and anger and clamor and slander be put away from you, along with all malice. Be kind to one another, tender-hearted, forgiving each other, just as God in Christ also has forgiven you" (Ephesians 4:31-32).

It Is Agreeing to Live with the Consequences of Someone Else's Sin
Jesus Christ took our sins upon Himself and bore the burden for the penalty of our sins. He voluntarily agreed to live with the consequences of our sins, knowing it would mean His death.

But it's not fair to have to live with something someone else has done! No, of course it's not fair, but we have to do it anyway. Everybody is living with the consequences of somebody else's sin. We are all living with the consequences of Adam's sin. The only real choice is to live with the consequences of their sin in the bondage of bitterness or in the freedom of forgiveness. "But where is the justice?" you might ask. It is in the cross of Jesus Christ, our Lord and Savior. He died once for all our sins: my sins, his sins, her sins, our sins and their sins. We will never have perfect justice in this lifetime. That is why we need to forgive and trust God that everything will be made equitable after the final judgment. Christians should work for justice wherever they go, but justice will never be perfect in human courts. Secular courts don't have the same moral standard that the Church has. Judges and juries never have the total picture as God does, and that is why they are incapable of perfect judgment.

Living with the consequences of another person's sin doesn't mean that we can't also take a stand for the sake of righteousness, carry out Church discipline or confront a brother who is sinning. It means that we don't let the sin of another person determine who we are, dictate how we are supposed to live or keep us in bondage.

Pause for Thought
Why can't you have justice in your lifetime? When should you keep seeking justice and when should you forgive and get on with your life?

It Is Letting God Be the Avenger

When we forgive others, we free ourselves from the bondage of bitterness that keeps us chained to them. This does not mean that God has let our offenders off the hook, though. Romans 12:19-21 reminds us:

> Never take your own revenge, beloved, but leave room for the wrath of God, for it is written, "Vengeance is mine, I will repay," says the Lord. "But if your enemy is hungry, feed him, and if he is thirsty, give him a drink; for in so doing you will heap burning coals on his head." Do not be overcome by evil, but overcome evil with good.

God will mete out justice in His time, which is usually later than we would like it. Our responsibility is to be like Christ and live out the law of love. "For the whole Law is fulfilled in one word, in the statement, 'You shall love your neighbor as yourself'" (Galatians 5:14).

We have the choice whether we are going to sin in return for their sin or love in return for their sin.

> Brethren, even if anyone is caught in any trespass, you who are spiritual, restore such a one in a spirit of gentleness; each one looking to yourself, so that you too will not be tempted. Bear one another's burdens, and thereby fulfill the law of Christ (Galatians 6:1-2).

The phrase "you who are spiritual" in this verse doesn't necessarily refer to our spiritual maturity. It refers to responding in the power of the Holy Spirit rather than responding in the flesh. The flesh will respond in anger, seek revenge, demand immediate justice and defend itself. When we are filled with the Holy Spirit, we will gently restore the offender. The burden that we are asked to carry consists of the consequences of their sin. That is the law of Christ as explained by Dietrich Bonhoeffer:

> The law of Christ, which it is our duty to fulfill, is the bearing of the cross. My brother's burden, which I must bear, is not only his outward lot, his natural characteristics and gifts, but quite literally his sin. And the only way to bear that sin is by forgiving it in the power of the cross of Christ in which I now share. Thus the call to follow Christ always means a call to share the work of forgiving men their sins. Forgiveness is the Christ-like suffering which it is the Christian's duty to bear.[1]

HOW TO FORGIVE FROM THE HEART

Whenever possible, minor offenses should be ignored. Imperfections are something we all have. Each of us has character flaws and bad moments that irritate others. We need to accept one another just as Christ accepted us (see Romans 15:7). Forgiveness is part of the Christian lifestyle. For these minor flaws and bad moments—while we may not be consciously thinking it—our actions should say, "It is okay that you are not perfect. I have no right to expect perfection from you because I am not perfect. Therefore, I forgive you for not being fully sanctified." In that way we model the unconditional love and acceptance of God.

Some offenses, however, cannot be overlooked. If we find ourselves becoming angry or offended by an individual's behavior, we are faced with the decision of whether we are going to forgive that person. Forgiveness is a crisis of the will, a decision to not seek revenge, live in resentment or remain bitter. It is a decision to live with the consequences of the offender's sin and not use the sin against that person in the future. It is a decision to be like Christ and to maintain communion with God.

The Healing Process

The truth is, we don't heal in order to forgive. We forgive in order to heal. The healing process cannot start and reconciliation cannot take place until we face the crisis of forgiveness. In the Steps to Freedom in Christ, we encourage people to pray and ask God to reveal to their minds exactly whom they need to forgive. He will, even in the face of denial (i.e., "There is no one I need to forgive."). If God has commanded us to do something, then by His grace He will enable us to do it. What is to be gained initially is freedom from past offenses and the freedom to be the people God has created us to be.

The Lord doesn't just provide names; He often brings up issues that have been buried in our subconscious. During the Steps to Freedom in Christ, we encourage counselors to stay with every person until every offense has been faced, whether it was a sin of commission or omission. For instance, "Lord, I forgive my father for verbally abusing me, which made me feel worthless and unloved." Adding how an offense made us feel helps us get in touch with our emotions. It is very hard, if not impossible, to forgive from the heart if we don't get in touch with our core emotions. After the counselors are through with each person, we close with the following prayer:

Lord, I choose not to hold on to my resentment. I thank You for setting me free from the bondage of my bitterness. I relinquish my right to seek revenge and ask You to heal my damaged emotions. I now ask You to bless those who have hurt me. In Jesus' name I pray, amen.

The Temptation to Revisit Old Pain

After we have forgiven from the heart, we will still be tempted from time to time to dwell on the offense. If we have successfully forgiven someone, we should be able to think about the person or see him or her without being emotionally overcome. This doesn't mean that we will *like* him or her; we can't be dishonest with how we feel and God isn't asking us to. Forgiveness allows us to go to the other person with purer motives—the love of Christ. If our purpose is not to restore the other person or be reconciled, then it is best we don't try to approach him or her. The decision to forgive is made every time we think about the abuse or see the person. To maintain our communion with God, we should develop a mental attitude that says, "Lord, I forgave that person and I am going to reject any bitter or hateful thoughts about him or her."

WITNESS

The following two questions will help participants begin to formulate ideas for sharing their faith with others. Invite volunteers to offer suggestions for witnessing to nonbelievers, and encourage participants to write down ideas in their student guide.

1. How might the issue of forgiveness challenge someone who is not yet a Christian?

2. How can you demonstrate forgiveness to someone who does not yet know the Lord?

GROUP DISCUSSION QUESTIONS

Instruct participants to form small groups of four to six, and assign each group several questions to discuss. Allow several minutes for discussion; then bring the whole group back together, and have volunteers from each small group share their group's questions and answers.

1. Do you agree that initially the crisis of forgiveness is between you and God rather than between you and the other person? Does it feel like that? Why?

2. Why is it important to make a distinction between seeking the forgiveness of others and forgiving others?

3. Define "justice," "mercy" and "grace," and illustrate how they should work out in our relationships with others.

4. What is the difference between forgiving and forgetting?

5. How can you forgive past abuse and set up scriptural boundaries to stop further abuse?

6. Who continues to feel pain when there is no forgiveness: the offender or the offended? Why?

7. How do we forgive from the heart?

8. What would you tell a person who refuses to forgive?

TAKING IT WITH YOU

The following information is included in the student guide and is intended for participants to use during the upcoming week. Direct participants to this section and encourage them to do the quiet-time suggestion and to consider the Big Question before the next session.

SUGGESTION FOR QUIET TIME

Review this lesson and look up the pertinent passages that teach about forgiveness. Ask the Holy Spirit to bring to your mind those whom you need to forgive from your heart.

THE BIG QUESTION

Before the next session, consider the following question:

How are we supposed to relate to others in terms of love, acceptance, judgment and discipline?

Note

1. Dietrich Bonhoeffer, *The Cost of Discipleship*, trans. R. H. Fuller, (New York: MacMillan, 1963), p. 100.

LEADING PEOPLE THROUGH THE STEPS TO FREEDOM IN CHRIST

THE LORD'S BOND-SERVANT MUST NOT BE QUARRELSOME, BUT BE KIND TO ALL, ABLE TO TEACH, PATIENT WHEN WRONGED, WITH GENTLENESS CORRECTING THOSE WHO ARE IN OPPOSITION, IF PERHAPS GOD MAY GRANT THEM REPENTANCE LEADING TO THE KNOWLEDGE OF THE TRUTH, AND THEY MAY COME TO THEIR SENSES AND ESCAPE FROM THE SNARE OF THE DEVIL, HAVING BEEN HELD CAPTIVE BY HIM TO DO HIS WILL.
2 TIMOTHY 2:24-26

SESSION OVERVIEW

OBJECTIVE

In this session, you will lead participants through a repentance process using the Steps to Freedom in Christ (the Steps). Through this process, participants will begin to resolve their personal and spiritual conflicts by submitting to God and resisting the devil (see James 4:7), thereby experiencing their freedom in Christ.

FOCUS TRUTH

Confession is the first step to repentance, but as Christians we must also make a choice about what we believe and how we live each day. If we want to grow in Christ, we must renounce the lies we have believed and any immorality in our lifestyles. We must announce our choice to believe what God says is true and then start living accordingly.

BRIEFING

Leading a group through the Steps will take approximately 90 minutes—however, you should allow two full hours. There are two options for leading participants through the Steps: (1) use the interactive DVD, or (2)

present the material yourself. For either option, you will need a meeting area large enough to afford some degree of privacy for each participant. You'll also need to make sure every participant has a copy of the *Beta Student Guide* (the Steps are located in the student guide, beginning on page 52).

1. **Using the DVD**—If you choose this option, you'll need the following materials:
   - DVD player
   - TV or video monitor positioned so that it is visible to the entire group
   - Pens or pencils
2. **Presenting the Material Yourself**—The Word portion of this lesson will give you some guidelines for this option. You'll also need pens or pencils.

Whichever method you choose for presenting the Steps, begin the session in prayer; then explain what will happen during the next two hours. Explain that many participants will get in touch with real pain and that tears are both understandable and acceptable. The group will be praying several prayers together out loud; then participants will be spending some time alone with God. Be sure to calm any fears of embarrassment by assuring participants that no one will be asked to share anything with the group or another person—their time during the Steps is *soleyan* (which means dedicated to a soul's encounter) with God.

Note: If you are leading your group through the Steps during a weekend retreat or have planned an extended session, include a time of sharing and worship before beginning the Steps.

BEGIN HERE
IF USING THE DVD

Turn on the DVD. It will begin with an overview of the Steps and the process participants will be going through. Each step will first be explained and then will begin with group prayer. When the prayer and final instructions for that particular step are finished, pause the DVD until everybody has finished that step. Allow a few minutes for each step and always ask if anyone needs more time. It is important to wait until everyone is finished. (**Note:** The Step on forgiveness is the longest, and you should allow at least 20 minutes.)

Note: If there are participants who are unable to go through the Steps on their own or taking a long time to process each Step, they need to set up a personal appointment with a trained encourager. The book *Discipleship Counseling* explains the theology of the Steps and how to guide someone through them.[1]

WORD

Important Note: The Word segment of this session is not for sharing with participants. It is for you as the leader to use as a reference tool should you choose to take your group through the Steps without using the DVD. We highly recommend that you watch the DVD prior to presenting the Steps to your group even if you are not going to use it with your group because it will help provide a model that you can follow.

PREPARING TO LEAD YOUR GROUP THROUGH THE STEPS TO FREEDOM IN CHRIST

Before the Cross, Satan was not a defeated foe, and the Church was not yet in existence. Believers had not yet been born again and were still living under the Law. Jesus clearly demonstrated His authority and power over the kingdom of darkness. Jesus conferred power and authority onto His 12 disciples (see Luke 9:1) and then onto the 70 (see Luke 10:1-20).

Pentecost came after the death, resurrection and ascension of Christ. Now every believer is a new creation in Christ and seated with Him in the heavenlies. The Church has been given the authority to continue the work of Christ, which includes setting captives free and binding up the brokenhearted. It is important to note, however, that the Church itself is not doing this; Christ is accomplishing it through the Church as long as believers remain dependent on Him.

Understand Casting Out Demons

There are no instructions in the Epistles for casting out demons because it is no longer the responsibility of an outside agent. As believers we each have the same standing in Christ, and we can't confess, repent, believe, renounce, forgive or assume any responsibility for another person. We can help others, however, and Paul shares how we can do this in 2 Timothy 2:24-26:

> The Lord's bond-servant must not be quarrelsome, but be kind to all, able to teach, patient when wronged, with gentleness correcting those who are in opposition, if perhaps God may grant them repentance leading to the knowledge of the truth, and they may come to their senses and escape from the snare of the devil, having been held captive by him to do his will.

This passage teaches us that truth sets us free and that God is the one who grants repentance. Christian counseling is an encounter with God—He is the wonderful counselor. Only He can bind up the brokenhearted and set the captives free. God does, however, work through His bond servants who are dependent on Him.

If you were successful in casting out a demon from someone without that person's involvement, what would keep the demon from coming back when you leave? Unless the individual assumes responsibility for his or her own freedom, that person may end up like the poor fellow who was freed from one spirit only to be occupied by seven others who were worse than the first (see Matthew 12:43-45)!

Some Christians have adopted their methodology from the Gospels and attempt to call up the demons, get their name and rank and cast them out. With this approach, the pastor or counselor is the deliverer and is getting information from a demon. We should never believe demons because they are all liars. "Whenever he speaks a lie, he speaks from his own nature, for he is a liar and the father of lies" (John 8:44).

The Epistles teach a different methodology. First, the deliverer is Christ—and He has already come. Second, we should get our information from the Word of God and the Holy Spirit, who will lead us into all truth.

If we try to resist the devil without first submitting to God, the result will be a dogfight. On the other hand, if we submit to God without resisting the devil, we will stay in bondage.

Realize That Truth Is Our Weapon

Setting Christians free is not a power encounter; it is a truth encounter. There is not a verse in the Bible that instructs us to pursue power because believers already have all the power we need through Christ (see Ephesians 1:18-19). The power for Christian living is found in the truth. Satan's only power is his ability to deceive, which is only effective in the dark, and all the darkness in the world cannot extinguish the light of one candle.

Satan's scare tactics are intended to provoke a fear response in us. Fear of the enemy and faith in God are mutually exclusive; when fear controls us, the Spirit of God does not. If we are not controlled by the Spirit of God, Satan has the upper hand.

More than anything else, Satan fears detection. Whenever the light of truth comes on, he and his demons, like cockroaches, head for the shadows. We should do what we can to prevent Satan from manifesting himself and glorifying himself through a power encounter. We are to glorify *God* by allowing *His* presence to be manifested. God does everything "properly and in an orderly manner" (1 Corinthians 14:40), and He is glorified when we maintain control of the whole process.

According to 2 Timothy 2:24-26, our primary qualification is to be "the Lord's bond-servant." To be an instrument in God's hand, we must be completely dependent on Him. Beyond that requirement, the Lord's bond servant must be kind, patient, gentle and able to teach. In other words, we need to know the truth and to speak the truth in love—because it is that truth that sets us free. Past traumas do not hold us in bondage; but rather, our believing in the lies that are a result of those traumas is what holds us in bondage.

A truth encounter has many specific advantages. First, it keeps a ministry from polarizing into psychotherapy that doesn't take into account the reality of the spiritual world. A truth encounter keeps the ministry from focusing on *deliverance* and neglecting to take into account psychological issues and personal responsibility. Any lasting answer must take into account *all* reality. Second, the method is transferable because it doesn't depend on gifts or calling. Third, it produces lasting results because the participants are the ones making the decisions and assuming personal responsibility, rather than the pastor or counselor doing it for them. Fourth, it doesn't bypass the person's mind. Fifth, the focus is on Christ and repentance. The real issue isn't Satan; it is God and our walk with Him. The seven Steps are seven issues that are critical in our relationship with God.

GUIDELINES FOR HELPING INDIVIDUALS THROUGH THE STEPS

The truth encounter requires the same personal skills needed for any other counseling procedure. As the leader, you must be compassionate, nonjudgmental and understanding. You must also be a good listener and empathetic. Solomon warned, "He who gives an answer before he hears, it is folly and shame to him" (Proverbs 18:13). Practically speaking, this means listening to someone's story before attempting to resolve his or her problem.

Gather Background Information

Churches prefer to use the term "encourager" instead of "counselor" and "freedom appointment" instead of "counseling session." This is done for liability purposes. There is a reproducible Confidential Personal Inventory in the appendix of *Discipleship Counseling*.[2] If you own a copy of the book, you have permission to copy the inventory or adapt it for your own use. Many people, however, will not disclose certain confidential information on a written sheet of paper. Choose a comfortable room and allow several hours for the freedom appointment, particularly if it is a difficult case. Have a box of tissues and some water nearby.

When the freedom appointment begins, you should first ask the participant for a brief family history by asking the following questions:

- What were the religious experiences of your parents or grandparents?
- Were your parents or grandparents involved in the occult or a counterfeit religion?
- Was there harmony in your home?
- Have there been any divorces or affairs in your family?

Dysfunction in families breeds false beliefs. For example, children whose parents divorce blame themselves for the breakup of the marriage. This blame can carry through to adulthood. Other adults continue to harbor bitterness toward their parents for something that happened in the home while they were growing up.

Additionally, you'll need to ask:

- Is there a history of alcoholism, drug abuse, sexual addiction or mental illness in your family?
- In what types of exercise and eating habits did you family engage?
- What was the moral climate of your home?

Ask the participant to share his or her early childhood and school experiences. Note that you are not trying to resolve anything by hearing their personal and family history. Instead, the purpose of getting the information is to understand what factors may have caused the participant to have certain beliefs. The intimate details will come out when you take the participant through the Steps.

The Confidential Personal Inventory previously mentioned will also provide important information concerning the participant's physical, mental, emotional and spiritual life.

Determine False Beliefs

Most people caught in a spiritual conflict have a distorted concept of God and themselves. It may be helpful in some cases to review from previous lessons the truth about God and who we are in Christ. Defeated Christians don't know who they are in Christ or understand what it means to be a child of God. Consequently, they question their salvation. Many think they are different from other people. The Christian life doesn't seem to work for them as it does for others. Some fear a mental breakdown and are filled with anxiety—almost all feel unloved, worthless and rejected. These Christians have tried everything they can think of to improve their self-image but have found nothing that works. Some even suspect that their problem is spiritual, but they don't know how to resolve their conflicts. It is hoped that the Beta course has already taught them the truth about who they are now in Christ.

Defeated Christians often have a distorted concept of the two kingdoms. They think they are caught between two opposite *but equal* powers—bad ol' Satan on one side, good ol' God on the other and the poor ol' Christian caught in the middle. That of course is not true, and they are only defeated as long as they believe that lie. The truth is that God is omnipresent, omnipotent and omniscient. Satan is a defeated foe, and we are alive in Christ, seated with Him in the heavenlies.

Deal with the Individual, Not the Demons

In difficult cases, Satan seems to be more present, real and powerful to people than God. These people usually hear opposing arguments in their head; and they are constantly confronted with lies, told to get out of the counseling session or threatened with harm or embarrassment.

Such mental interference is not uncommon, and this is why you should explain that the mind is the control center. If the participant doesn't lose control in his or her mind, you will not lose control in the freedom appointment. In one sense, it doesn't matter whether the negative or condemning thoughts are coming from a speaker on the wall, from the participant's own memory or even from the pit of hell. The only way those thoughts can have any control over the participant is if he or she believes them. To help maintain mental control, ask the participant to share what is going on in his or her mind. Bring the deceptive thoughts into the light, expose the lie, and the power will be broken.

The participant may be reluctant to share with you for two reasons: (1) he or she may not think you will believe what you are told; or (2) the voices heard are too intimidating and are threatening to harm the participant, the encourager or family and friends.

If the participant is hearing voices, secular counselors and many Christian counselors don't consider the voices to be demonic. The participant would be given a psychological label and a prescription for medication. Realizing this, the troubled person may share what has happened but may be very reluctant to share the mental battle that is going on inside his or her head.

Watch the participant's eyes very carefully. If they start to become dizzy, glassy-eyed, or if the participant starts looking around the room, stop what you are doing and ask him or her to share what is going on inside. If you aren't paying attention, you could lose control of the session. If the participant is really struggling mentally, encourage him or her to get up and go for a walk. You want the participant to know that he or she has a choice and can exercise his or her will.

Highly subjective people have negative thoughts and act on them without realizing it. They don't seem to realize they have a will or can say no to negative thoughts. Instruct your participant by saying, "If you have a thought, don't act on it. Share it with me." That is revolutionary for some people. Highly subjective people are the most difficult to help because they have never really assumed responsibility for their own thoughts.

To help maintain control in the freedom appointment, the Steps begin with a very specific prayer and declaration. If the participant has made a declaration of faith in God, Satan cannot touch him or her because he has no authority over that person.

Don't touch the participant during a freedom appointment if he or she has been abused in the past. This can cause the participant to feel violated. People still under demonic oppression will recoil and move away from you. After they are free, however, just the opposite happens; they will move toward you. Opposite spirits repel, but the Holy Spirit unites.

Never try to restrain anyone physically, because the weapons of our warfare are not of the flesh (2 Corinthians 10:3-4). If the participant runs out of the room or office, allow him or her to do so. Wait and pray, and inevitably the participant will come back, usually within five minutes. Never violate his or her mind or try to control the person. The participant must be free to stay or leave.

If the person you are trying to help has been actively involved in satanism, be prepared for major opposition. There is an appendix in the Steps that has special renunciations for those who have worshiped Satan or been subjected to satanic ritual abuse. Everything they do is an antithesis of Christianity because Satan is the antichrist. It could take you several hours to work through those renunciations. Paul wrote, "Let us cleanse ourselves from all defilement of flesh and spirit, perfecting holiness in the fear of God" (2 Corinthians 7:1). Rebuilding someone's fractured God concept and self-concept takes time, lots of love and acceptance and the support of an understanding Christian community. Paul summarized this ministry in 2 Corinthians 4:1-4:

> Therefore, since we have this ministry, as we received mercy, we do not lose heart, but we have renounced the things hidden because of shame, not walking in craftiness or adulterating the word of God, but by the manifestation of truth commending ourselves to every man's conscience in the sight of God. And even if our gospel is veiled, it is veiled to those who are perishing, in whose case the god of this world has blinded the minds of the unbelieving so that they might not see the light of the gospel of the glory of Christ, who is the image of God.

Lead the Individual Through the Steps to Freedom

The Steps to Freedom in Christ don't set you free; the Steps are tools that can be used rightly or wrongly. Our response to Christ in repentance and faith sets us free. The primary focus of the Steps is our relationship with God. Many people can and do go through the Steps on their own. The process is different from most counseling approaches because the one who is praying is the one who needs the help, and that person is praying to the only One who can help him or her.

The process of submitting to God and resisting the devil is not that difficult. God made some of us smart and some of us not so smart. Don't believe that His grace is available only to the smart. Those who think they are smart should seek to make the plan of Christian living so easy to understand—without being simplistic—that anyone who desires to understand it can.

Suppose you were hopelessly lost in a maze. Would you want a mazeologist to explain all the intricacies of the maze and teach you coping skills so you can survive in the maze? Would you want a sick legalistic preacher calling you a jerk for getting lost in the maze? I think you would want to know the way, the truth and the life. The paths back to God can't be that numerous. Actually there is only one way. There are a million ways to sin, but the answer is the same. You could be abused a thousand different ways, but you would still need to forgive the abuser for your own sake.

The participant also has a copy of the Steps. Explain the Steps—what they are and why they are necessary. Try to go through all seven steps in one session. The participant may not need every step, but you want to be thorough for his or her sake. Have him or her read every prayer and doctrinal affirmation aloud. It is hoped that the participant will share any mental opposition or physical discomfort. When this happens, thank him or her for sharing it with you, and then once it is acknowledged, simply go on. In most cases there is very little opposition. Spiritual opposition usually shows up only in the first two steps.

Forgiveness is the most critical of the Steps. Every person has at least one person—and usually several people—to forgive. Unforgiveness affords the biggest door to the Church for Satan. If you can't help a person forgive from the heart, you can't help that person to be freed from his or her past.

When a participant prays and asks God whom he or she needs to forgive, rest assured that God will bring names to that person's mind. If the participant says, "I can't think of anyone," you should respond by asking, "Would you just share the names that are coming to your mind right now?" Without exception several names will surface, and you should record them on a sheet of paper. It is not uncommon for participants to have names come to mind that surprise them, and it is not uncommon for them to recall forgotten painful memories while in the process of forgiving.

Explain what forgiveness is and how to do it. The key issues are highlighted in the Steps. After explaining, give the list to the participant and ask if he or she would be willing to forgive those people for his or her own sake. Forgiving others is primarily an issue between us and our heavenly Father. Reconciliation may or may not follow.

Very little opposition occurs during steps 4 through 6. In step 6, deal with sexual sins separately. It is amazing how much sexual sins have a part in human bondage. There are several prayers that the participant could pray in step 6 for specific issues. Ask if any are pertinent to the participant.

In most cases, complete freedom isn't realized until after the final declaration and prayer in step 7. When finished, ask the participant to sit comfortably and close his or her eyes, and then ask, "What do you hear in your mind? Is it quiet?" After a pause, the participant will most likely respond with a relieved smile and say something like, "Nothing. It's finally quiet in my mind." If the participant had difficulty reading the doctrinal affirmation in step 2, have him or her read it again. You will see that he or she can hardly believe the ease with which it can now be read and the truth understood. The countenance of many participants often changes so markedly that you may want them to look at themselves in a mirror.

Getting free in Christ is one thing; staying free is another. Paul said in Galatians 5:1, "It was for freedom that Christ set us free; therefore keep standing firm and do not be subject again to a yoke of slavery." The Steps include several aftercare suggestions that will help participants maintain their freedom in Christ. Freedom in Christ Ministries has prepared a 21-day devotional book entitled *Walking in Freedom,* which we encourage everyone to work through.[3] Every third day, one of the Steps is repeated, and this helps reinforce what the participant has done.

Notes
1. Dr. Neil T. Anderson, *Discipleship Counseling* (Ventura, CA: Regal Books, 2003).
2. Ibid.
3. Dr. Neil T. Anderson, *Walking in Freedom* (Ventura, CA: Regal Books, 1999).

THE STEPS TO FREEDOM IN CHRIST

THE WHOLE GOSPEL

God created Adam and Eve to be spiritually alive, which means that their souls were in union with God. Living in a dependent relationship with their heavenly Father, they were to exercise dominion over the earth. Acting independently of God, they chose to disobey Him and their choice to sin separated them from God. Consequently, all their descendants are born physically alive but spiritually dead—separated from God. Since we have all sinned and fallen short of the glory of God (see Romans 3:23), we remain separated from Him and cannot fulfill the original purpose for our creation, which is to glorify God and enjoy His presence forever. Satan became the rebel holder of authority and the god of this world. Jesus referred to him as the ruler of this world, and the apostle John wrote that the whole world lies in the power of the evil one (see 1 John 5:19).

Jesus came to undo the works of Satan (see 1 John 3:8) and to take upon Himself the sins of the world. By dying for our sins, Jesus removed the enmity that existed between God and those He created in His image. The resurrection of Christ brought new life to those who put their trust in Him. Every born-again believer's soul is again in union with God and that is most often communicated in the New Testament as being "in Christ," or "in Him." The apostle Paul explained that anyone who is *in Christ* is a new creation (see 2 Corinthians 5:17). The apostle John wrote, "But as many as received Him, to them He gave the right to become children of God, even to those who believe in His name" (John 1:12), and he also wrote, "See how great a love the Father has bestowed on us, that we would be called children of God; and such we are" (1 John 3:1).

No amount of effort on your part can save you and neither can any religious activity no matter how well intentioned. We are saved by faith and by faith alone. All that remains for us to do is put our trust in the finished work of Christ. "For by grace you have been saved through faith; and that not of yourselves, it is the gift of God; not as a result of works, so that no one may boast" (Ephesians 2:8-9). If you have never received Christ, you can do so right now. God knows the thoughts and intentions of your heart, so all you have to do is put your trust

in God alone. You can express your decision in prayer as follows:

Dear Heavenly Father, thank You for sending Jesus to die on the cross for my sins. I acknowledge that I have sinned and that I cannot save myself. I believe that Jesus came to give me life, and by faith I now choose to receive You into my life as my Lord and Savior. By the power of Your indwelling presence enable me to be the person You created me to be. I pray that You would grant me repentance leading to a knowledge of the truth so that I can experience my freedom in Christ and be transformed by the renewing of my mind. In Jesus' precious name I pray. Amen.

ASSURANCE OF SALVATION

Paul wrote, "If you confess with your mouth Jesus as Lord, and believe in your heart that God raised Him from the dead, you will be saved" (Romans 10:9). Do you believe that God the Father raised Jesus from the dead? Did you invite Jesus to be your Lord and Savior? Then you are a child of God, and nothing can separate you from the love of Christ (see Romans 8:35). Your heavenly Father has sent His Holy Spirit to live within you and bear witness with your spirit that you are a child of God (see Romans 8:16). "You were sealed *in Him* with the Holy Spirit of promise" (Ephesians 1:13, emphasis added). The Holy Spirit will guide you into all truth (see John 16:13).

RESOLVING PERSONAL AND SPIRITUAL CONFLICTS

Since we all were born spiritually dead in our trespasses and sin (see Ephesians 2:1), we had neither the presence of God in our lives nor the knowledge of His ways. Consequently, we all learned to live our lives independently of God. When we became new creations in Christ, our minds were not instantly renewed. That is why Paul wrote, "Do not be conformed any longer to this world, but be transformed by the renewing of your mind" (Romans 12:2).

Then you will be able to test and approve what God's will is—His good, pleasing, and perfect will (see Romans 12:2). That is why new Christians struggle with many of the same old thoughts and habits. Their minds have been previously programmed to live independently of God and that is the chief characteristic of our old nature or flesh. As new creations in Christ, we have the mind of Christ, and the Holy Spirit will lead us into all truth.

To experience our freedom in Christ and to grow in the grace of God require repentance, which literally means a change of mind. Repentance is not something we can do on our own; therefore, we need to submit to God and resist the devil (see James 4:7). The Steps to Freedom in Christ (the Steps) are designed to help you do that. Submitting to God is the critical issue. He is the wonderful counselor and the One who grants repentance leading to a knowledge of the truth (see 2 Timothy 2:24-26). The Steps cover seven critical issues between ourselves and God. We will not experience our freedom in Christ if we seek false guidance, believe lies, fail to forgive others as we have been forgiven, live in rebellion, respond in pride, fail to acknowledge our sin and continue in the sins of our ancestors. "He who conceals his transgressions will not prosper, but he who confesses and forsakes [renounces] them will find compassion" (Proverbs 28:13). "Therefore since we have this ministry, as we received mercy, we do not lose heart, but we have renounced things hidden because of shame, not walking in craftiness or adulterating the word of God, but by the manifestation of truth" (2 Corinthians 4:1-2).

Even though Satan is defeated, he still rules this world through a hierarchy of demons who tempt, accuse and deceive those who fail to put on the armor of God, stand firm in their faith and take every thought captive to the obedience of Christ. Our sanctuary is our identity and position in Christ, and we have all the protection we need to live victorious lives; but if we fail to assume our responsibility and give ground to Satan, we will suffer the consequences of our sinful attitudes and actions. The good news is, we can repent and reclaim all that we have in Christ, and that is what the Steps will enable you to do.

PROCESSING THE STEPS

Ideally, it would be best if you read *Victory over the Darkness* and *The Bondage Breaker* before you process the Steps.[1] Audio books and audiocassettes are also available from Freedom in Christ Ministries. The best way to go through the Steps is to process them with a trained encourager. The book *Discipleship Counseling* explains the theology and process.[2] You can also go through the Steps on your own. Every step is explained so that you will have no trouble doing that. I suggest you find a quiet place where you can process the Steps out loud. If you experience some mental interference, just ignore it and continue on. Thoughts such as *This isn't going to work* or *I don't believe this*, or blasphemous, condemning and accusing thoughts have no power over you unless you believe them. They are just thoughts and it doesn't make any difference if they originate from yourself, an external source or from Satan and his demons. Such thoughts will be resolved when you have fully repented. If you are working with a trained encourager, share any mental or physical opposition that you are experiencing. The mind is the control center, and you will not lose control in the freedom appointment if you don't lose control of your mind. The best way to do that, if you are being mentally harassed, is to just share it. Exposing the lies to the light breaks the power of the darkness.

Remember, you are a child of God and seated with Christ in the heavenlies. That means you have the authority and power to do His will. The Steps don't set you free. Jesus sets you free, and you will progressively experience that freedom as you respond to Him in faith and repentance. Don't worry about any demonic interference; most do not experience any. It doesn't make any difference if Satan has a little role or a bigger role; the critical issue is your relationship with God and that is what you are resolving. This is a ministry of reconciliation. Once those issues are resolved, Satan has no right to remain. Successfully completing this repentance process is not an end; but rather, it is the beginning of growth. Unless these issues are resolved, however, the growth process will be stalled and your Christian life will be stagnant.

PREPARATION

Processing the Steps can play a major role in your continuing process of discipleship. The purpose is to get you firmly rooted in Christ. It doesn't take long to establish your identity and freedom in Christ, but there is no such thing as instant maturity. Renewing your mind and conforming to the image of God is a lifelong process. May the Lord grace you with His presence as you seek to do His will. Once you have experienced your freedom in Christ, you can help others experience the joy of their salvation. Begin the Steps with the following prayer and declaration:

PRAYER

Dear Heavenly Father, You are present in this room and in my life. You alone are all-knowing, all-powerful and everywhere present, and I worship You alone. I declare my dependency on You, for apart from You I can do nothing. I choose to believe Your Word which teaches that all authority in heaven and on Earth belongs to the resurrected Christ, and being alive in Christ I have the authority to resist the devil as I submit to You. I ask that You fill me with Your Holy Spirit and guide me into all truth. I ask for Your complete protection and guidance as I seek to know You and do Your will. In the wonderful name of Jesus, I pray. Amen.

DECLARATION

In the name and authority of the Lord Jesus Christ, I command Satan and all evil spirits to release their hold on me in order that I can be free to know and choose to do the will of God. As a child of God who is seated with Christ in the heavenly places, I declare that every enemy of the Lord Jesus Christ in my presence be bound. Satan and all his demons cannot inflict any pain or in any way prevent God's will from being done in my life today because I belong to the Lord Jesus Christ.

REVIEW OF YOUR LIFE

Before going through the Steps, review the following events of your life to discern specific areas that need to be addressed:

FAMILY HISTORY

❑ Religious history of parents and grandparents

❑ Home life from childhood through high school

❑ History of physical or emotional illness in the family

❑ Adoption, foster care, guardians

PERSONAL HISTORY

❑ Eating habits (bulimia, anorexia, compulsive eating)

❑ Addictions (cigarettes, drugs, alcohol)

❑ Prescription medications (what for?)

❑ Sleeping patterns, dreams and nightmares

❑ Rape or any other sexual, physical or emotional abuse

❑ Thought life (obsessive, blasphemous, condemning and distracting thoughts; poor concentration; fantasy; suicidal thoughts; fearful; jealous; confused; guilt and shame)

❑ Mental interference during church, prayer or Bible study

❑ Emotional life (anger, anxiety, depression, bitterness and fear)

❑ Spiritual journey (salvation: when, how and assurance)

Notes

1. Neil T. Anderson, *Victory over the Darkness* (Ventura, CA: Regal Books, 2000); Neil T. Anderson, *The Bondage Breaker* (Eugene, OR: Harvest House, 2000).
2. Neil T. Anderson, *Discipleship Counseling* (Ventura, CA: Regal Books, 2003).

COUNTERFEIT VERSUS REAL

The first step toward experiencing your freedom in Christ is to renounce (verbally reject) all involvement (past or present) with occult, cult or false religious teachings or practices. Participation in any group that denies that Jesus Christ is Lord and/or elevates any teaching or book to the level of (or above) the Bible must be renounced. In addition, groups that require dark, secret initiations, ceremonies, vows, pacts or covenants need to be renounced. God does not take lightly false guidance. "As for the person who turns to mediums and to spiritists . . . I will also set My face against that person and will cut him off from among his people" (Leviticus 20:6). Since you don't want the Lord to cut you off, ask Him to guide you as follows:

Dear Heavenly Father, please bring to my mind anything and everything that I have done knowingly or unknowingly that involves occult, cult, false religious teachings or practices. I want to experience Your freedom by renouncing any and all false guidance. In Jesus' name I pray. Amen.

The Lord may bring things to your mind that you had forgotten, even things you participated in as a game or thought were jokes. You might even have been passively yet curiously watching others participate in counterfeit religious practices. The purpose is to renounce all counterfeit spiritual experiences and their beliefs.

To help bring these things to your mind, prayerfully consider the following Non-Christian Spiritual Checklist. Then pray the prayer following the checklist to renounce each activity or group the Lord brings to mind. He may reveal to you ones that are not on the list. Be especially aware of your need to renounce non-Christian folk religious practices if you have grown up in another culture. It is important that you prayerfully renounce them **out loud**.

NON-CHRISTIAN SPIRITUAL CHECKLIST

(Check all in which you have participated.)

- ❑ Out-of-body experience
- ❑ Ouija board
- ❑ Bloody Mary
- ❑ Occult games
- ❑ Magic Eight Ball
- ❑ Spells or curses
- ❑ Mental telepathy/control
- ❑ Automatic writing
- ❑ Trances
- ❑ Spirit guides
- ❑ Fortune-telling/divination
- ❑ Tarot cards
- ❑ Levitation
- ❑ Witchcraft/wicca/sorcery
- ❑ Satanism
- ❑ Palm reading
- ❑ Astrology/horoscopes

- ❑ Hypnosis
- ❑ Astral projection
- ❑ Seances/mediums/channelers
- ❑ Black or white magic
- ❑ Blood pacts
- ❑ Fetishism/crystals/charms
- ❑ Sexual spirits
- ❑ Martial arts (mysticism)
- ❑ Superstitions
- ❑ Mormonism (Latter-day Saints)
- ❑ Jehovah's Witness
- ❑ New Age (teachings, medicine)
- ❑ Masons
- ❑ Christian Science/Mind Science
- ❑ Unification Church (Moonies)
- ❑ The Forum (EST)
- ❑ Church of Scientology
- ❑ Unitarianism/Universalism

- ❑ Silva Mind Control
- ❑ Transcendental Meditation (TM)
- ❑ Yoga (religion, not the exercise)
- ❑ Hare Krishna
- ❑ Bahaism
- ❑ Native American spirit worship
- ❑ Islam
- ❑ Hinduism
- ❑ Buddhism (including Zen)
- ❑ Black Muslim
- ❑ Rosicrucianism
- ❑ False gods (money, sex, power, pleasure, certain people)
- ❑ Other (non-Christian religions; cults; movies; music; books; video games; comics or fantasy games that glorify Satan, which precipitated nightmares or mental battles; and all other questionable spiritual experiences including spiritual visitations and nightmares)

Additional Questions to Help You Become Aware of Counterfeit Religious Experiences

1. Do you now have, or have you ever had, an imaginary friend, spirit guide or angel offering you guidance or companionship? (If it has a name, renounce it by name.)

2. Have you ever heard voices in your head or had repeating, nagging thoughts (such as *I'm dumb, I'm ugly, Nobody loves me* or *I can't do anything right*) as if there were a conversation going on inside your head?

3. Have you ever been hypnotized, attended a New Age seminar or consulted a medium or spiritist?

4. Have you ever made a secret vow or pact (or inner vow; i.e., *I will never . . .*)?

5. Have you ever been involved in a satanic ritual or attended a concert or event in which Satan was the focus?

Once you have completed your checklist and the questions, confess and renounce every false religious practice, belief, ceremony, vow or pact in which you were involved by praying the following prayer **aloud:**

> **Lord Jesus, I confess that I have participated in** [specifically name every belief and involvement related to all that you have checked above], **and I renounce them all as counterfeits. I pray that You will fill me with Your Holy Spirit so that I may be guided by You. Thank You that in Christ I am forgiven. Amen.**

SATANIC WORSHIP

People who have been subjected to Satanic Ritual Abuse (SRA) need the help of someone who understands dissociative disorders and spiritual warfare. If you have been involved in any form of satanic worship, say **aloud** the following Special Renunciations. Read across the page, renouncing the first item in the column entitled "Kingdom of Darkness," and then announcing the truth in the column entitled "Kingdom of Light." Continue down the page in this manner. Notice that satanic worship is the antithesis of true worship.

Kingdom of Darkness	Kingdom of Light
I renounce ever signing my name over to Satan or having my name signed over to Satan.	I announce that my name is now written in the Lamb's book of life.
I renounce any ceremony in which I have been wed to Satan.	I announce that I am the bride of Christ.
I renounce any and all covenants I made with Satan.	I announce that I am under the new covenant with Christ.
I renounce all satanic assignments for my life, including duties, marriage and children.	I announce and commit myself to know and do only the will of God and accept only His guidance.
I renounce all spirit guides assigned to me.	I accept only the leading of the Holy Spirit.
I renounce ever giving my blood in the service of Satan.	I trust only the blood of the Lord Jesus Christ.
I renounce ever eating flesh or drinking blood for satanic worship.	By faith I symbolically eat only the flesh and drink only the blood of Jesus in Holy Communion.
I renounce any and all guardians and satanist parents who were assigned to me.	I announce that God is my Father and the Holy Spirit is my guardian by whom I am sealed.
I renounce any baptism whereby I have been identified with Satan.	I announce that I have been baptized into Christ Jesus.
I renounce any and all sacrifices that were made on my behalf by which Satan may claim ownership of me.	I announce that only the sacrifice of Christ has any hold on me. I belong to Him. I have been purchased by the blood of the Lamb.

DECEPTION VERSUS TRUTH

The Christian life is lived by faith according to what God says is true. Jesus is the truth, the Holy Spirit is the Spirit of truth, God's Word is truth, and we are to speak the truth in love (see John 14:6; 16:13; 17:17; Ephesians 4:15). The biblical response to truth is *faith*, regardless of whether we *feel* it is true. In addition, Christians are to have no part in lying, deceiving, stretching the truth, or anything else associated with falsehood. Lies keep us in bondage, but it is the truth that sets us free (see John 8:32). David wrote, "How blessed [happy] is the man . . . in whose spirit there is no deceit" (Psalm 32:2). Joy and freedom come from walking in the truth.

We find the strength to walk in the light of honesty and transparency before God and others (see 1 John 1:7) when we know that God loves and accepts us just as we are. We can face reality, acknowledge our sins and not try to hide. Begin this commitment to truth by praying the following prayer **aloud**. Don't let any opposing thoughts, such as *This is a waste of time* or *I wish I could believe this, but I can't*, keep you from pressing forward. God will strengthen you as you rely on Him.

> **Dear Heavenly Father, You are the truth and I desire to live by faith according to Your truth. The truth will set me free, but in many ways I have been deceived by the father of lies and the philosophies of this fallen world, and I have deceived myself. I choose to walk in the light, knowing that You love and accept me just as I am. As I consider areas of possible deception, I invite the Spirit of truth to guide me into all truth. Please protect me from all deception as You "search me, O God, and know my heart; try me and know my anxious thoughts; and see if there be any hurtful way in me, and lead me in the everlasting way" [Psalm 139:23-24]. In the name of Jesus, I pray. Amen.**

Prayerfully consider the lists in the following three exercises, using the prayer at the end of each exercise in order to confess any ways you have given in to deception or wrongly defended yourself. You cannot instantly renew your mind, but the process will never begin unless you acknowledge your mental strongholds or defense mechanisms, which are sometimes called flesh patterns.

WAYS YOU CAN BE DECEIVED BY THE WORLD

- ❏ Believing that acquiring money and things will bring lasting happiness (see Matthew 13:22; 1 Timothy 6:10)
- ❏ Believing that excessive food and alcohol can relieve your stress and make you happy (see Proverbs 23:19-21)
- ❏ Believing that an attractive body and personality will get you what you need (see Proverbs 31:30; 1 Peter 3:3-4)
- ❏ Believing that gratifying sexual lust will bring lasting satisfaction (see Ephesians 4:22; 1 Peter 2:11)
- ❏ Believing that you can sin and get away without any negative consequences (see Hebrews 3:12-13)
- ❏ Believing that you need more than what God has given you in Christ (see 2 Corinthians 11:2-4,13-15)
- ❏ Believing that you can do whatever you want and no one can touch you (see Proverbs 16:18; Obadiah 3; 1 Peter 5:5)
- ❏ Believing that unrighteous people who refuse to accept Christ go to heaven anyway (see 1 Corinthians 6:9-11)
- ❏ Believing that you can associate with bad company and not become corrupted (see 1 Corinthians 15:33-34)
- ❏ Believing that you can read, see or listen to anything and not be corrupted (see Proverbs 4:23-27; Matthew 5:28)
- ❏ Believing that there are no consequences on Earth for your sin (see Galatians 6:7-8)
- ❏ Believing that you must gain the approval of certain people in order to be happy (see Galatians 1:10)
- ❏ Believing that you must measure up to certain standards in order to feel good about yourself (see Galatians 3:2-3; 5:1)

> **Lord Jesus, I confess that I have been deceived by** [confess the items you checked above]. **I thank You for Your forgiveness, and I commit myself to believe only Your truth. In Jesus' name I pray. Amen.**

WAYS YOU DECEIVE YOURSELF

❏ Hearing God's Word but not doing what it says (see James 1:22)

❏ Saying you have no sin (see 1 John 1:8)

❏ Thinking you are something you are really not (see Galatians 6:3)

❏ Thinking you are wise in this worldly age (see 1 Corinthians 3:18-19)

❏ Thinking you can be truly religious but not bridle your tongue (see James 1:26)

❏ Thinking that God is the source of your problems (see Lamentations 3)

❏ Thinking you can live your life without the help of anyone else (see 1 Corinthians 12:14-20)

Lord Jesus, I confess that I have deceived myself by [confess the items checked above]. **Thank You for Your forgiveness. I commit myself to believe only Your truth. In Jesus' name I pray. Amen.**

WAYS YOU WRONGLY DEFEND YOURSELF

❏ Denial of reality (conscious or unconscious)

❏ Fantasy (escaping reality by daydreaming, TV, movies, music, computer or video games, drugs, alcohol)

❏ Emotional insulation (withdrawing from people or keeping people at a distance to avoid rejection)

❏ Regression (reverting back to less threatening times)

❏ Displaced anger (taking out frustrations on innocent people)

❏ Projection (attributing to another what you find unacceptable in yourself)

❏ Rationalization (making excuses for your own poor behavior)

❏ Lying (protecting yourself through falsehoods)

❏ Blaming yourself (when you are not responsible) and others

❏ Hypocrisy (presenting a false image)

Lord Jesus, I confess that I have wrongly defended myself by [confess the items checked above]. **Thank You for Your forgiveness. I trust You to defend and protect me. In Jesus' name I pray. Amen.**

The wrong ways we have employed to shield ourselves from pain and rejection are often deeply ingrained in our lives. You may need additional discipling or counseling to learn how to allow Christ to be your rock, fortress, deliverer and refuge (see Psalm 18:1-2). The more you learn how loving, powerful and protective God is, the more you'll be likely to trust Him. The more you realize His complete acceptance of you in Christ, the more you'll be released to be open, honest and (in a healthy way) vulnerable before God and others.

The New Age movement has twisted the concept of faith by teaching that we make something true by believing it. That is false. We cannot create reality with our minds; only God can do that. Our responsibility is to *face* reality and choose to believe what God says is true. True biblical faith, therefore, is choosing to believe and act upon what is true, because God has said it is true, and He is the Truth. Faith is something you decide to do, not something you feel like doing. Believing something doesn't make it true; *it's already true, therefore we choose to believe it!*

Everybody lives by faith. The only difference between Christian faith and non-Christian faith is the object of our faith. If the object of our faith is not trustworthy, then no amount of believing will change that. That's why our faith must be grounded on the solid rock of God's perfect, unchanging character and the truth of His Word. For two thousand years Christians have known the importance of verbally and publicly declaring truth.

Read **aloud** the following Statements of Truth, and carefully consider what you are professing. You may find it helpful to read them **aloud** daily for several weeks, which will help renew your mind to the truth.

STATEMENTS OF TRUTH

1. I recognize that there is only one true and living God who exists as the Father, Son and Holy Spirit. He is worthy of all honor, praise and glory as the One who made all things and holds all things together. [See Exodus 20:2-3; Colossians 1:16-17.]

2. I recognize Jesus Christ as the Messiah, the Word who became flesh and dwelt among us. I believe that He came to destroy the works of the devil and that He disarmed the rulers and authorities and made a public display of them, having triumphed over them. [See John 1:1,14; Colossians 2:15; 1 John 3:8.]

3. I believe that God demonstrated His own love for me in that while I was still a sinner, Christ died for me. I believe that He has delivered me from the domain of darkness and transferred me to His kingdom, and in Him I have redemption, the forgiveness of sins. [See Romans 5:8; Colossians 1:13-14.]

4. I believe that I am now a child of God and that I am seated with Christ in the heavenlies. I believe that I was saved by the grace of God through faith and that it was a gift and not a result of any works on my part. [See Ephesians 2:6,8-9; 1 John 3:1-3.]

5. I choose to be strong in the Lord and in the strength of His might. I put no confidence in the flesh, for the weapons of warfare are not of the flesh but are divinely powerful for the destruction of strongholds. I put on the full armor of God. I resolve to stand firm in my faith and resist the evil one. [See 2 Corinthians 10:4; Ephesians 6:10-20; Philippians 3:3.]

6. I believe that apart from Christ I can do nothing, so I declare my complete dependence on Him. I choose to abide in Christ in order to bear much fruit and glorify my Father. I announce to Satan that Jesus is my Lord. I reject any and all counterfeit gifts or works of Satan in my life. [See John 15:5,8; 1 Corinthians 12:3.]

7. I believe that the truth will set me free and that Jesus is the truth. If He sets me free, I will be free indeed. I recognize that walking in the light is the only path of true fellowship with God and man. Therefore, I stand against all of Satan's deception by taking every thought captive in obedience to Christ. I declare that the Bible is the only authoritative standard for truth and life. [See John 8:32,36; 14:6; 2 Corinthians 10:5; 2 Timothy 3:15-17; 1 John 1:3-7.]

8. I choose to present my body to God as a living and holy sacrifice and the members of my body as instruments of righteousness. I choose to renew my mind by the living Word of God in order that I may prove that the will of God is good, acceptable and perfect. I put off the old self with its evil practices and I put on the new self. I declare myself to be a new creation in Christ. [See Romans 6:13; 12:1-2; 2 Corinthians 5:17; Colossians 3:9-10.]

9. By faith, I choose to be filled with the Spirit so that I can be guided into all truth. I choose to walk by the Spirit so that I will not carry out the desires of the flesh. [See John 16:13; Galatians 5:16; Ephesians 5:18.]

10. I renounce all selfish goals and choose the ultimate goal of love. I choose to obey the two greatest commandments: to love the Lord my God with all my heart, soul, mind and strength and to love my neighbor as myself. [See Matthew 22:37-39; 1 Timothy 1:5.]

11. I believe that the Lord Jesus has all authority in heaven and on Earth, and He is the head over all rule and authority. I am complete in Him. I believe that Satan and his demons are subject to me in Christ since I am a member of Christ's Body. Therefore, I obey the command to submit to God and resist the devil, and I command Satan in the name of Jesus Christ to leave my presence. [See Matthew 28:18; Ephesians 1:19-23; Colossians 2:10; James 4:7.]

BITTERNESS VERSUS FORGIVENESS

We are called to be merciful just as our heavenly Father is merciful (see Luke 6:36) and forgive others as we have been forgiven (see Ephesians 4:31-32). Doing so sets us free from our past and doesn't allow Satan to take advantage of us (see 2 Corinthians 2:10-11). Ask God to bring to your mind the people you need to forgive by praying the following prayer **aloud:**

Dear Heavenly Father, I thank You for the riches of Your kindness, forbearance and patience toward me, knowing that Your kindness has led me to repentance. I confess that I have not shown that same kindness and patience toward those who have hurt or offended me [see Romans 2:4]. **Instead, I have held on to my anger, bitterness and resentment toward them. Please bring to my mind all the people I need to forgive in order that I may now do so. In Jesus' name I pray. Amen.**

On a separate sheet of paper, list the names of people who come to your mind. At this point don't question whether you need to forgive them. Often we hold things against ourselves as well, punishing ourselves for wrong choices we've made in the past. Write "myself" at the bottom of your list if you need to forgive yourself. Forgiving yourself is accepting the truth that God has already forgiven you in Christ. If God forgives you, you can forgive yourself!

Also write down "Thoughts Against God" at the bottom of your list. Obviously, God has never done anything wrong, so He doesn't need our forgiveness; but we need to let go of our disappointments with our heavenly Father. People often harbor angry thoughts against Him because He did not do what they wanted Him to do. Those feelings of anger or resentment toward God need to be released.

Before you begin working through the process of forgiving those on your list, review what forgiveness is and what it is not. The critical points are highlighted in bold print.

- **Forgiveness is not forgetting.** People who want to forget all that was done to them will find they cannot do it. When God says that He will "not remember your sins" (Isaiah 43:25), He is saying that He will not use the past against us. Forgetting is a long-term by-product of forgiveness, but it is never a means toward it. Don't put off forgiving those who have hurt you, hoping the pain will go away. Once you choose to forgive someone, *then* Christ will heal your wounds. We don't heal in order to forgive; we forgive in order to heal.

- **Forgiveness is a choice, a decision of the will.** Since God requires you to forgive, it is something you can do. Some people hold on to their anger as a means of protecting themselves against further abuse, but all they are doing is hurting themselves. Others want revenge. The Bible teaches, "'Vengeance is mine, I will repay,' says the Lord" (Romans 12:19). Let God deal with the person. Let him or her off your hook because as long as you refuse to forgive someone, you are still hooked to that person. You are still chained to your past, bound up in your bitterness. By forgiving, you let the other person off your hook, but he or she is not off God's hook. You must trust that God will deal with the person justly and fairly, something you simply cannot do.

  But you don't know how much this person hurt me! No other human really knows another person's pain, but Jesus does, and He instructed us to forgive others for our sake. Until you let go of your bitterness and hatred, the person is still hurting you. Nobody can fix your past, but you can be free from it. What you gain by forgiving is freedom from your past and those who have abused you. To forgive is to set a captive free and then realize you were the captive.

- **Forgiveness is agreeing to live with the consequences of another person's sin.** We are all living with the consequences of someone else's sin. The only choice is whether to do so in the *bondage of bitterness* or in the *freedom of forgiveness.* But where is the justice? The Cross makes forgiveness legally and morally right. Jesus died, once for all our sins. We are to forgive as Christ has forgiven us. He did that by taking upon Himself the consequences of our sins. God "made Him who knew no sin to be sin on our behalf, so that we might become the righteousness of God in

Him" (2 Corinthians 5:21). Do not wait for the other person to ask for your forgiveness. Remember, Jesus did not wait for those who were crucifying Him to apologize before He forgave them. Even while they mocked and jeered at Him, He prayed, "Father, forgive them; for they do not know what they are doing" (Luke 23:34).

- **Forgive from your heart.** Allow God to bring to the surface the painful memories and acknowledge how you feel toward those who've hurt you. If your forgiveness doesn't touch the emotional core of your life, it will be incomplete. Too often we're afraid of the pain, so we bury our emotions deep down inside us. Let God bring them to the surface, so He can begin to heal those damaged emotions.

- **Forgiveness is choosing not to hold someone's sin against him or her anymore.** It is common for bitter people to bring up past offenses with those who have hurt them. They want them to feel as bad as they do! But we must let go of the past and choose to reject any thought of revenge. This doesn't mean you continue to put up with the abuse. God does not tolerate sin and neither should you. You will need to set up scriptural boundaries that put a stop to further abuse. Take a stand against sin while continuing to exercise grace and forgiveness toward those who hurt you. If you need help setting scriptural boundaries to protect yourself from further abuse, talk to a trusted friend, counselor or pastor.

- **Don't wait until you feel like forgiving.** You will never get there. Make the hard choice to forgive, even if you don't feel like it. Once you choose to forgive, Satan will lose his hold on you, and God will heal your damaged emotions.

Start with the first person on your list, and make the choice to forgive him or her for every painful memory that comes to your mind. Stay with that individual until you are sure you have dealt with all the remembered pain. Then work your way down the list in the same way.

As you begin forgiving people, God may bring to your mind painful memories that you've totally forgotten. Let Him do this, even if it hurts. God is surfacing those painful memories so that you can face them once for all time and let them go. Don't excuse the offender's behavior, even if it is someone you are really close to.

Don't say, "Lord, please help me to forgive." He is already helping you and will be with you all the way through the process. Don't say, "Lord, I want to forgive," because that bypasses the hard choice we have to make. Say, "Lord, I choose to forgive these people and what they did to me."

For every painful memory that God reveals for each person on your list, pray **aloud:**

> **Lord Jesus, I choose to forgive** [name the person] **for** [what he or she did or failed to do] **because it made me feel** [share the painful feelings; i.e., rejected, dirty, worthless, inferior, etc.].

After you have forgiven every person for every painful memory, then pray as follows:

> **Lord Jesus, I choose not to hold on to my resentment. I relinquish my right to seek revenge and ask You to heal my damaged emotions. Thank You for setting me free from the bondage of my bitterness. I now ask You to bless those who have hurt me. In Jesus' name I pray. Amen.**

Before we came to Christ, thoughts were raised up in our minds against a true knowledge of God (see 2 Corinthians 10:3-5). Even as believers we have harbored resentments toward God and that will hinder our walk with Him. We should have a healthy fear of God—awe of His holiness, power and presence—but we fear no punishment from Him. Romans 8:15 reads, "For you have not received a spirit of slavery leading to fear again, but you have received a spirit of adoption as sons by which we cry out, 'Abba! Father!'"

The following exercise will help renew your mind to a true knowledge of your heavenly Father. Read the list **aloud** starting with the left column and then reading the corresponding right column. Begin each one with the statement in bold at the top of that list.

ACKNOWLEDGING THE TRUTH ABOUT YOUR FATHER GOD

I renounce the lie that my Father God is	I choose to believe the truth that my Father God is
Distant and disinterested	**Intimate and involved** [see Psalm 139:1-18]
Insensitive and uncaring	**Kind and compassionate** [see Psalm 103:8-14]
Stern and demanding	**Accepting and filled with joy and love** [see Zephaniah 3:17; Romans 15:7]
Passive and cold	**Warm and affectionate** [see Isaiah 40:11; Hosea 11:3-4]
Absent or too busy for me	**Always with me and eager to be with me** [see Jeremiah 31:20; Ezekiel 34:11-16; Hebrews 13:5]
Impatient, angry and rejecting	**Patient and slow to anger** [see Exodus 34:6; 2 Peter 3:9]
Mean, cruel or abusive	**Loving, gentle and protective** [see Jeremiah 31:3; Isaiah 42:3; Psalm 18:2]
Trying to take all the fun out of life	**Trustworthy and wants to give me a full life; His will is good, perfect and acceptable for me** [see Lamentations 3:22-23; John 10:10; Romans 12:1-2]
Controlling or manipulative	**Full of grace and mercy, and He gives me freedom to fail** [see Luke 15:11-16; Hebrews 4:15-16]
Condemning or unforgiving	**Tenderhearted and forgiving; His heart and arms are always open to me** [see Psalm 130:1-4; Luke 15:17-24]
A nit-picking, demanding perfectionist	**Committed to my growth and proud of me as His beloved child** [see Romans 8:28-29; Hebrews 12:5-11; 2 Corinthians 7:4]

I AM THE APPLE OF HIS EYE!
(SEE DEUTERONOMY 32:9-10.)

STEP 4

REBELLION VERSUS SUBMISSION

We live in rebellious times. Many people sit in judgment of those in authority over them, and they submit only when it is convenient, or they do so in the fear of being caught. The Bible instructs us to pray for those in authority over us (see 1 Timothy 2:1-2) and to submit to governing authorities (see Romans 13:1-7). Rebelling against God and His established authority leaves us spiritually vulnerable. The only time God permits us to disobey earthly leaders is when they require us to do something morally wrong or attempt to rule outside the realm of their authority. To have a submissive spirit and servant's heart, pray the following prayer **aloud:**

Dear Heavenly Father, You have said that rebellion is as the sin of witchcraft and insubordination is as iniquity and idolatry [see 1 Samuel 15:23]. **I know that I have not always been submissive but instead have rebelled in my heart against You and against those You have placed in authority over me in attitude and in action. Please show me all the ways I have been rebellious. I choose now to adopt a submissive spirit and a servant's heart. In Jesus' name I pray. Amen.**

It is an act of faith to trust God to work in our lives through something less than perfect leaders, but that is what God is asking us to do. Should those in positions of leadership or power abuse their authority and break the laws designed to protect innocent people, you need to seek help from a higher authority. Many states require certain types of abuse to be reported to a governmental agency. If that is your situation, we urge you to get the help you need immediately. Don't, however, assume that someone in authority is violating God's Word just because he or she is telling you to do something you don't like. God has set up specific lines of authority to protect us and give order to society. It is the position of authority that we respect. Without governing authorities every society would be chaos. From the list below, allow the Lord to show you any specific ways you have been rebellious and use the prayer that follows to confess those sins He brings to mind.

- ❑ Civil government, including traffic laws, tax laws, attitude toward government officials (see Romans 13:1-7; 1 Timothy 2:1-4; 1 Peter 2:13-17)
- ❑ Parents, stepparents or legal guardians (see Ephesians 6:1-3)
- ❑ Teachers, coaches and school officials (see Romans 13:1-4)
- ❑ Employers—past and present (see 1 Peter 2:18-23).
- ❑ Husband (see 1 Peter 3:1-4) or wife (see Ephesians 5:21; 1 Peter 3:7)
  (**Note to Husbands:** Ask the Lord if your lack of love for your wife could be fostering a rebellious spirit within her. If so, confess that as a violation of Ephesians 5:22-33.)
- ❑ Church leaders (see Hebrews 13:7)
- ❑ God (see Daniel 9:5,9)

For each way in which the Spirit of God brings to your mind that you have been rebellious, use the following prayer to specifically confess that sin:

Lord Jesus, I confess that I have been rebellious toward [name or position] **by** [specifically confess what you did or did not do]. **Thank You for Your forgiveness. I choose to be submissive and obedient to Your Word. In Jesus' name I pray. Amen.**

PRIDE VERSUS HUMILITY

Pride comes before a fall, but God gives grace to the humble (see James 4:6; 1 Peter 5:1-10). Humility is confidence properly placed in God, and we are instructed to "put no confidence in the flesh" (Philippians 3:3). We are to be "strong in the Lord and in the strength of His might" (Ephesians 6:10). Proverbs 3:5-7 urges us to trust in the Lord with all our hearts and to not lean on our own understanding. Use the following prayer to ask for God's guidance concerning ways that you may be prideful:

Dear Heavenly Father, You have said that pride goes before destruction and an arrogant spirit before stumbling. I confess that I have focused on my own needs and desires and not others'. I have not always denied myself, picked up my cross daily and followed You. I have relied on my own strength and resources instead of resting in Yours. I have placed my will before Yours and centered my life around myself instead of You. I confess my pride and selfishness and pray that all ground gained in my life by the enemies of the Lord Jesus Christ would be canceled. I choose to rely upon the Holy Spirit's power and guidance so that I will do nothing from selfishness or empty conceit. But with humility of mind, I choose to regard others as more important than myself. I acknowledge You as my Lord, and I confess that apart from You I can do nothing of lasting significance. Please examine my heart and show me the specific ways I have lived my life in pride. In the gentle and humble name of Jesus, I pray. Amen. [See Proverbs 16:18; Matthew 6:33; 16:24; Romans 12:10; Philippians 2:3.]

Pray through the following list and then pray the prayer to confess any sins of pride the Lord brings to mind:

❏ Having a stronger desire to do my will than God's will

❏ Leaning too much on my own understanding and experience rather than seeking God's guidance through prayer and His Word

❏ Relying on my own strengths and resources instead of depending on the power of the Holy Spirit

❏ Being more concerned about controlling others than in developing self-control

❏ Being too busy doing seemingly important and selfish things rather than seeking and doing God's will

❏ Having a tendency to think that I have no needs

❏ Finding it hard to admit when I am wrong

❏ Being more concerned about pleasing people than pleasing God

❏ Being overly concerned about getting the credit I feel I deserve

❏ Thinking I am more humble, spiritual, religious or devoted than others

❏ Being driven to obtain recognition by attaining degrees, titles and positions

❏ Often feeling that my needs are more important than another person's needs

❏ Considering myself better than others because of my academic, artistic or athletic abilities and accomplishments

❏ Having feelings of inferiority appearing as false humility

❏ Not waiting on God

❏ Other ways I have thought more highly of myself than I should

For each of the above areas that has been true in your life, pray **aloud:**

Lord Jesus, I agree I have been proud by [name each item you checked above]. Thank You for Your forgiveness. I choose to humble myself before You and others. I choose to place all my confidence in You and not to put confidence in my flesh. In Jesus' name I pray. Amen.

STEP 6

BONDAGE VERSUS FREEDOM

Many times we feel trapped in a vicious cycle of sin-confess-sin-confess that never seems to end. We can become very discouraged and end up just giving up and giving in to the sins of the flesh. In order to experience our freedom, we must follow James 4:7: "Submit therefore to God. Resist the devil and he will flee from you." We submit to God by confession of sin and repentance (turning away from sin). We resist the devil by rejecting his lies. We must walk in the truth and put on the full armor of God (see Ephesians 6:10-20).

Sin that has become a habit often may require help from a trusted brother or sister in Christ. James 5:16 says, "Confess your sins to one another, and pray for one another so that you may be healed. The effective prayer of a righteous man can accomplish much." Sometimes the assurance of 1 John 1:9 is enough: "If we confess our sins, He is faithful and righteous to forgive us our sins and to cleanse us from all unrighteousness."

Remember, confession is not just saying, "I'm sorry." It is openly admitting, "I did it." Whether you need help from other people or just the accountability of walking in the light before God, pray the following prayer **aloud:**

Dear Heavenly Father, You have told me to put on the Lord Jesus Christ and make no provision for the flesh in regard to its lust. I confess that I have given in to fleshly lusts that wage war against my soul. I thank You that in Christ my sins are already forgiven, but I have broken Your holy law and I have allowed sin to wage war in my body. I come to You now to confess and renounce these sins of the flesh so that I might be cleansed and set free from the bondage of sin. Please reveal to my mind all the sins of the flesh I have committed and the ways I have grieved the Holy Spirit. In Jesus' holy name I pray. Amen. [See Romans 6:12-13; 13:14; 2 Corinthians 4:2; James 4:1; 1 Peter 2:11; 5:8.]

The following list contains many sins of the flesh, but a prayerful examination of Mark 7:20-23; Galatians 5:19-21; Ephesians 4:25-31 and other Scripture passages will help you to be even more thorough. Look over the list below and the Scriptures just listed, and ask the Holy Spirit to bring to your mind the sins you need to confess. He may reveal others to you as well. For each one the Lord shows you, pray a prayer of confession from your heart. There is a sample prayer following the list. (**Note:** Sexual sins, eating disorders, substance abuse, abortion, suicidal tendencies and perfectionism will be dealt with later in this step. Further counseling may be necessary to find complete healing and freedom in these and other areas.)

❑ Stealing	❑ Swearing	❑ Cheating
❑ Quarreling/fighting	❑ Apathy/laziness	❑ Procrastination
❑ Jealousy/envy	❑ Lying	❑ Greed/materialism
❑ Complaining/criticism	❑ Hatred	❑ Others:
❑ Sarcasm	❑ Anger	_____
❑ Lustful actions	❑ Lustful thoughts	_____
❑ Gossip/slander	❑ Drunkenness	_____

Lord Jesus, I confess that I have sinned against You by [name the sins]. **Thank You for Your forgiveness and cleansing. I now turn away from these expressions of sin and turn to You, Lord. Fill me with Your Holy Spirit so that I will not carry out the desires of the flesh. In Jesus' name I pray. Amen.**

Note: If you are struggling with habitual sin, read Neil T. Anderson and Mike Quarles, *Overcoming Addictive Behavior* (Ventura, CA: Regal Books, 2003).

RESOLVING SEXUAL SIN

It is our responsibility not to allow sin to reign (rule) in our mortal bodies. We must not use our bodies or another person's body as an instrument of unrighteousness (see Romans 6:12-13). Sexual immorality is not only a sin against God, but also it is a sin against your body, the temple of the Holy Spirit (see 1 Corinthians 6:18-19). To find freedom from sexual bondage, begin by praying the following prayer:

> **Lord Jesus, I have allowed sin to reign in my mortal body. I ask You to bring to my mind every sexual use of my body as an instrument of unrighteousness so that I can renounce these sexual sins and break those sinful bondages. In Jesus' name I pray. Amen.**

As the Lord brings to your mind every immoral sexual use of your body, whether it was done to you (rape, incest, sexual molestation) or willingly by you (pornography, masturbation, sexual immorality), renounce *every* experience as follows:

> **Lord Jesus, I renounce** [name the sexual experience] **with** [name]. **I ask You to break that sinful bond with** [name] **spiritually, physically and emotionally.**

After you are finished, commit your body to the Lord by praying:

> **Lord Jesus, I renounce all these uses of my body as an instrument of unrighteousness, and I admit to any willful participation. I choose to present my physical body to You as an instrument of righteousness, a living and holy sacrifice, acceptable to You. I choose to reserve the sexual use of my body for marriage only. I reject the devil's lie that my body is not clean or that it is dirty or in any way unacceptable to You as a result of my past sexual experiences. Lord, thank You that You have cleansed and forgiven me and that You love and accept me just the way I am. Therefore, I choose now to accept myself and my body as clean in Your eyes. In Jesus' name I pray. Amen.**

Prayers for Specific Issues
Pornography

> **Lord Jesus, I confess that I have looked at sexually suggestive and pornographic material for the purpose of stimulating myself sexually. I have attempted to satisfy my lustful desires and polluted my body, soul and spirit. Thank You for cleansing me and for Your forgiveness. I renounce any satanic bonds I have allowed in my life through the unrighteous use of my body and mind. Lord, I commit myself to destroy any objects in my possession that I have used for sexual stimulation, and to turn away from all media that are associated with my sexual sin. I commit myself to the renewing of my mind and to thinking pure thoughts. Fill me with Your Holy Spirit so that I may not carry out the desires of the flesh. In Jesus' name I pray. Amen.**

Homosexuality

> **Lord Jesus, I renounce the lie that You have created me or anyone else to be homosexual, and I agree that in Your Word You clearly forbid homosexual behavior. I choose to accept myself as a child of God and I thank You that You created me as a man** [woman]. **I renounce all homosexual thoughts, urges, drives and acts, and I renounce all ways that Satan has used these things to pervert my relationships. I announce that I am free in Christ to relate to the opposite sex and my own sex in the way that You intended. In Jesus' name I pray. Amen.**

Abortion

Lord Jesus, I confess that I was not a proper guardian and keeper of the life You entrusted to me, and I confess that I have sinned. Thank You that because of Your forgiveness, I can forgive myself. I commit the child to You for all eternity and believe that he or she is in Your caring hands. In Jesus' name I pray. Amen.

Suicidal Tendencies

Lord Jesus, I renounce all suicidal thoughts and any attempts I've made to take my own life or in any way injure myself. I renounce the lie that life is hopeless and that I can find peace and freedom by taking my own life. Satan is a thief and comes to steal, kill and destroy. I choose life in Christ, who said He came to give me life and give it abundantly [see John 10:10]. Thank You for Your forgiveness that allows me to forgive myself. I choose to believe that there is always hope in Christ and that my heavenly Father loves me. In Jesus' name I pray. Amen.

Drivenness and Perfectionism

Lord Jesus, I renounce the lie that my sense of worth is dependent on my ability to perform. I announce the truth that my identity and my sense of worth are found in who I am as Your child. I renounce seeking the approval and acceptance of other people, and I choose to believe that I am already approved and accepted in Christ because of His death and resurrection for me. I choose to believe the truth that I have been saved, not by deeds done in righteousness, but according to Your mercy. I choose to believe that I am no longer under the curse of the Law because Christ became a curse for me. I receive the free gift of life in Christ and choose to abide in Him. I renounce striving for perfection by living under the Law. By Your grace, Heavenly Father, I choose from this day forward to walk by faith in the power of Your Holy Spirit according to what You have said is true. In Jesus' name I pray. Amen.

Eating Disorders or Self-Mutilation

Lord Jesus, I renounce the lie that my value as a person is dependent on my appearance or performance. I renounce cutting or abusing myself, vomiting, using laxatives or starving myself as a means of being in control, altering my appearance or trying to cleanse myself of evil. I announce that only the blood of the Lord Jesus Christ cleanses me from sin. I realize I have been bought with a price and my body, the temple of the Holy Spirit, belongs to God. Therefore, I choose to glorify God in my body. I renounce the lie that I am evil or that any part of my body is evil. Thank You that You accept me just the way I am in Christ. In Jesus' name I pray. Amen.

Substance Abuse

Lord Jesus, I confess that I have misused substances [alcohol, tobacco, food, prescription or street drugs] for the purpose of pleasure, to escape reality or to cope with difficult problems. I confess that I have abused my body and programmed my mind in harmful ways. I have quenched the Holy Spirit as well. Thank You for Your forgiveness. I renounce any satanic connection or influence in my life through my misuse of food or chemicals. I cast my anxieties on Christ who loves me. I commit myself to yield no longer to substance abuse, but instead I choose to allow the Holy Spirit to direct and empower me. In Jesus' name I pray. Amen.

Overcoming Fear

Fear is a God-given natural response when our physical or psychological safety is threatened. Courage is not the absence of fear, but it is living by faith and doing what is right in the face of illegitimate fear objects. The fear of God is the beginning of wisdom and the only fear that can overcome all other fears. Irrational fears compel us to live irresponsible lives or prevent us from doing that which is responsible and from being good witnesses. Behind every irrational fear is a lie that must be identified. Allow the Lord to surface any controlling fears in your life and any root lies by praying the following prayer:

Dear Heavenly Father, I confess that I have allowed fear to control me and that lack of faith is sin. Thank You for Your forgiveness. I recognize that You have not given me a spirit of fear, but of power, love and discipline [see 2 Timothy 1:7]. **I renounce any spirit of fear operating in my life and ask You to reveal any and all controlling fears in my life and the lies behind them. I desire to live by faith in You and in the power of the Holy Spirit. In Jesus' name I pray. Amen.**

❑ Fear of death

❑ Fear of never loving or being loved

❑ Fear of Satan

❑ Fear of embarrassment

❑ Fear of failure

❑ Fear of being victimized

❑ Fear of rejection by other people

❑ Fear of marriage

❑ Fear of disapproval

❑ Fear of divorce

❑ Fear of becoming/being homosexual

❑ Fear of going crazy

❑ Fear of financial problems

❑ Fear of pain/illness

❑ Fear of never getting married

❑ Fear of the future

❑ Fear of the death of a loved one

❑ Fear of confrontation

❑ Fear of being a hopeless case

❑ Fear of specific individuals (List them.)

_____

_____

_____

❑ Fear of losing my salvation

❑ Fear of not being loved by God

❑ Fear of having committed the unpardonable sin

❑ Other specific fears that come to mind now

_____

_____

_____

Analyze Your Fear

When did you first experience the fear, and what events preceded the first experience? What lies have you been believing that are the basis for the fear? How has the fear kept you from living a responsible life or compromised your witness? Confess any active or passive way that you have allowed fear to control you. Work out a plan of responsible behavior, and determine in advance what your response will be to any fear object. Commit yourself to follow through with your plan. If you do the thing you fear the most, the death of fear is certain.

Lord Jesus, I renounce the fear of [name the fear and associated lies] **because God has not given me a spirit of fear. I choose to live by faith in You, and I acknowledge You as the only legitimate fear object in my life. In Jesus' name I pray. Amen.**

Note: For additional help with fear, read Neil T. Anderson and Rich Miller, *Freedom from Fear* (Eugene, OR: Harvest House Publishers, 1999).

STEP 7

CURSES VERSUS BLESSINGS

Scripture declares that the iniquities of one generation can be visited on the third and fourth generations, but God's blessings will be poured out on thousands of generations of those who love and obey Him (see Exodus 20:4-6). The iniquities of one generation can adversely affect future ones unless those sins are renounced, and your new spiritual heritage in Christ is claimed. This cycle of abuse and all negative influences can be stopped through genuine repentance. Jesus died for your sins, but that is only appropriated when you choose to believe Him and only experienced when you repent. You are not guilty of your ancestors' sins, but because of their sins, you have been affected by their influence. Jesus said that after we have been fully trained we will be like our teachers (see Luke 6:40), and Peter wrote that you were redeemed "from your futile way of life inherited from your forefathers" (1 Peter 1:18). Ask the Lord to reveal your ancestral sins and then renounce them as follows:

> **Dear Heavenly Father, please reveal to my mind all the sins of my ancestors that have been passed down through family lines. Since I am a new creation in Christ, I want to experience my freedom from these influences and walk in my new identity as a child of God. In Jesus' name I pray. Amen.**

> **Lord, I renounce** [confess all the family sins that God brings to your mind].

Satan and people may curse us, but it will not have any effect on us unless we believe it. We cannot passively take our place in Christ—we must actively and intentionally choose to submit to God and to resist the devil, and then the devil will flee from us. Complete this final step with the following declaration and prayer:

DECLARATION

I here and now reject and disown all the sins of my ancestors. As one who has been delivered from the domain of darkness and transferred into the kingdom of God's Son, I declare myself to be free from those harmful influences. I am no longer "in Adam." I am now alive "in Christ." Therefore, I am the recipient of the blessings of God upon my life as I choose to love and obey Him. As one who has been crucified and raised with Christ and who sits with Him in heavenly places, I renounce any and all satanic attacks and assignments directed against me and my ministry. Every curse placed on me was broken when Christ became a curse for me by dying on the cross [see Galatians 3:13]. **I reject any and every way in which Satan may claim ownership of me. I belong to the Lord Jesus Christ who purchased me with His own precious blood. I declare myself to be fully and eternally signed over and committed to the Lord Jesus Christ. Therefore, having submitted to God and by His authority, I now resist the devil, and I command every spiritual enemy of the Lord Jesus Christ to leave my presence. I put on the armor of God and I stand against Satan's temptations, accusations and deceptions. From this day forward I will seek to do only the will of my heavenly Father.**

PRAYER

Dear Heavenly Father, I come to You as Your child, bought out of slavery to sin by the blood of the Lord Jesus Christ. You are the Lord of the universe and the Lord of my life. I submit my body to You as a living and holy sacrifice. May You be glorified through my life and body. I now ask You to fill me with Your Holy Spirit. I commit myself to the renewing of my mind in order that I may prove that Your will is good, acceptable and perfect for me. I desire nothing more than to be like You. I pray, believe and do all this in the wonderful name of Jesus, my Lord and Savior. Amen.

MAINTAINING YOUR FREEDOM

It is exciting to experience your freedom in Christ, but what you have gained must be maintained. You have won an important battle, but the war goes on. To maintain your freedom in Christ and grow in the grace of God, you must continue renewing your mind according to the truth of God's Word. If you become aware of lies that you have believed, renounce them and choose the truth. If more painful memories surface, then forgive those who hurt you and renounce any sinful part you played. Many people choose to go through the Steps again on their own to make sure they have dealt with all their issues. Oftentimes new issues will surface. The process can assist you when you do a regular house-cleaning.

It is not uncommon after going though the Steps for people to have thoughts such as *Nothing has really changed*; *I'm the same person I always was* or *It didn't work*. In most cases you should just ignore these thoughts. We are not called to dispel the darkness; we are called to turn on the light. You don't get rid of negative thoughts by rebuking every one; you get rid of them by repenting and choosing the truth.

I encourage you to read the books *Victory over the Darkness* and *The Bondage Breaker* if you haven't already done so in preparation for going through the Steps. The 21-day devotional *Walking in Freedom* was written for those who have completed the Steps.[1] If you want to continue growing in the grace of God, I also suggest the following:

- Get rid of or destroy any cult or occult objects in your home (see Acts 19:18-20).
- Get involved in a small-group ministry where you can be a real person, and be part of a church where God's truth is taught with kindness and grace.
- Read and meditate on the truth of God's Word each day.
- Don't let your mind be passive, especially concerning what you watch and listen to (music, TV, etc.). Actively take every thought captive to the obedience of Christ.
- Learn to pray by the Spirit (for information, read *Praying by the Power of the Spirit*).[2]
- Remember, you are responsible for your mental, spiritual and physical health (for more information on the latter, read *The Biblical Guide to Alternative Medicine*).[3]
- Work through the *Freedom in Christ Bible*, a discipleship study Bible that takes you through the sanctifying process five days a week for a year.[4]

DAILY PRAYER AND DECLARATION

Dear Heavenly Father, I praise You and honor You as my Lord and Savior. You are in control of all things. I thank You that You are always with me and will never leave me nor forsake me. You are the only all-powerful and only wise God. You are kind and loving in all Your ways. I love You and thank You that I am united with Christ and spiritually alive in Him. I choose not to love the world or the things in the world, and I crucify the flesh and all its passions.

Thank You for the life I now have in Christ. I ask You to fill me with the Holy Spirit so that I can be guided by You and not carry out the desires of the flesh. I declare my total dependence on You, and I take my stand against Satan and all his lying ways. I choose to believe the truth of God's Word despite what my feelings may say. I refuse to be discouraged; You are the God of all hope. Nothing is too difficult for You. I am confident that You will supply all my needs as I seek to live according to Your Word. I thank You that I can be content and live a responsible life through Christ who strengthens me.

I now take my stand against Satan and command him and all his evil spirits to depart from me. I choose to put on the full armor of God so that I may be able to stand firm against all the devil's schemes. I submit my body as a living and holy sacrifice to You, and I choose to renew my mind by Your living Word. By so doing I will be able to prove that Your will is good, acceptable and perfect for me. In the name of my Lord and Savior, Jesus Christ, I pray. Amen.

BEDTIME PRAYER

Thank You, Lord, that You have brought me into Your family and have blessed me with every spiritual blessing in the heavenly places in Christ Jesus. Thank You for this time of renewal and refreshment through sleep. I accept it as one of Your blessings for Your children, and I trust You to guard my mind and my body during my sleep.

As I have thought about You and Your truth during the day, I choose to let those good thoughts continue in my mind while I am asleep. I commit myself to You for Your protection against every attempt of Satan and his demons to attack me during sleep. Guard my mind from nightmares. I renounce all fear and cast every anxiety upon You, Lord. I commit myself to You as my rock, my fortress and my strong tower. May Your peace be upon this place of rest. In the strong name of the Lord Jesus Christ I pray. Amen.

PRAYER FOR SPIRITUAL CLEANSING OF HOME, APARTMENT OR ROOM

After removing and destroying all objects of false worship, pray this prayer **aloud** in every room:

Heavenly Father, I acknowledge that You are the Lord of heaven and Earth. In Your sovereign power and love, You have entrusted me with many things. Thank You for this place to live. I claim my home as a place of spiritual safety for me and my family and ask for Your protection from all the attacks of the enemy. As a child of God, raised up and seated with Christ in the heavenly places, I command every evil spirit claiming ground in this place, based on the activities of past or present occupants, including me and my family, to leave and never return. I renounce all demonic assignments directed against this place. I ask You, Heavenly Father, to post Your holy angels around this place to guard

it from any and all attempts of the enemy to enter and disturb Your purposes for me and my family. I thank You, Lord, for doing this in the name of the Lord Jesus Christ. Amen.

PRAYER FOR LIVING IN A NON-CHRISTIAN ENVIRONMENT

After removing and destroying all objects of false worship in your possession, pray this **aloud** in the place where you live:

Thank You, heavenly Father, for a place to live and to be renewed by sleep. I ask You to set aside my room [or portion of this room] as a place of spiritual safety for me. I renounce any allegiance given to false gods or spirits by other occupants. I renounce any claim to this room [space] by Satan based on the activities of past or present occupants, including me. On the basis of my position as a child of God and joint heir with Christ, who has all authority in heaven and on Earth, I command all evil spirits to leave this place and never return. I ask You, Heavenly Father, to station Your holy angels to protect me while I live here. In Jesus' mighty name I pray. Amen.

Paul prays in Ephesians 1:18, "I pray that the eyes of your heart may be enlightened, so that you will know what is the hope of His calling, what are the riches of the glory of His inheritance in the saints, and what is the surpassing greatness of His power toward us who believe." Beloved, you are a child of God (see 1 John 3:1-3), and "My God will supply all your needs according to His riches in glory in Christ Jesus" (Philippians 4:19). The critical needs are the "being" needs such as eternal or spiritual life that He has given you and the identity that you have in Christ. In addition, Jesus has met your needs for *acceptance, security* and *significance*. Memorize and meditate on the following truths daily. Read the entire list **aloud**, morning and evening, for the next few weeks. Think about what you are reading and let the truth of who you are in Christ renew your mind. This is your inheritance in Christ.

IN CHRIST

I renounce the lie that I am rejected, unloved or shameful. In Christ *I am accepted.* God says

- **I am God's child** [see John 1:12].
- **I am Christ's friend** [see John 15:5].
- **I have been justified** [see Romans 5:1].
- **I am united with the Lord, and I am one spirit with Him** [see 1 Corinthians 6:17].
- **I have been bought with a price. I belong to God** [see 1 Corinthians 6:19-20].
- **I am a member of Christ's Body** [see 1 Corinthians 12:27].
- **I am a saint, a holy one** [see Ephesians 1:1].
- **I have been adopted as God's child** [see Ephesians 1:5].
- **I have direct access to God through the Holy Spirit** [see Ephesians 2:18].
- **I have been redeemed and forgiven of all my sins** [see Colossians 1:14].
- **I am complete in Christ** [see Colossians 2:10].

I renounce the lie that I am guilty, unprotected, alone or abandoned. In Christ *I am secure.* God says

- **I am free from condemnation** [see Romans 8:1-2].
- **I am assured that all things work together for good** [see Romans 8:28].
- **I am free from any condemning charges against me** [see Romans 8:31-34].
- **I cannot be separated from the love of God** [see Romans 8:35-39].
- **I have been established, anointed and sealed by God** [see 2 Corinthians 1:21-22].
- **I am confident that the good work God has begun in me will be perfected** [see Philippians 1:6].

- **I am a citizen of heaven** [see Philippians 3:20].
- **I am hidden with Christ in God** [see Colossians 3:3].
- **I have not been given a spirit of fear but of power, love and discipline** [see 2 Timothy 1:7].
- **I can find grace and mercy to help in time of need** [see Hebrews 4:16].
- **I am born of God and the evil one cannot touch me** [see 1 John 5:18].

I renounce the lie that I am worthless, inadequate, helpless or hopeless. In Christ *I am significant.* God says

- **I am the salt of the earth and the light of the world** [see Matthew 5:13-14].
- **I am a branch of the true vine, Jesus, a channel of His life** [see John 15:1,5].
- **I have been chosen and appointed by God to bear fruit** [see John 15:16].
- **I am a personal, Spirit-empowered witness of Christ's** [see Acts 1:8].
- **I am a temple of God** [see 1 Corinthians 3:16].
- **I am a minister of reconciliation for God** [see 2 Corinthians 5:17-21].
- **I am God's coworker** [see 2 Corinthians 6:1].
- **I am seated with Christ in the heavenly realm** [see Ephesians 2:6].
- **I am God's workmanship, created for good works** [see Ephesians 2:10].
- **I may approach God with freedom and confidence** [see Ephesians 3:12].
- **I can do all things through Christ who strengthens me** [see Philippians 4:13]!

**I AM NOT THE GREAT "I AM,"
BUT BY THE GRACE OF GOD I AM WHO I AM.**
[SEE EXODUS 3:14; JOHN 8:24,28,58;
1 CORINTHIANS 15:10.]

Notes
1. Neil T. Anderson, *Walking in Freedom* (Ventura, CA: Regal Books, 1999).
2. Neil T. Anderson, *Praying by the Power of the Spirit* (Eugene, OR: Harvest House, 2003).
3. Neil T. Anderson and Michael Jacobson, *The Biblical Guide to Alternative Medicine* (Ventura, CA: Regal Books, 2003).
4. Neil T. Anderson, gen. ed., *Freedom in Christ Bible* (Grand Rapids, MI: Zondervan Publishing House, 2001).

GODLY RELATIONSHIPS

AND HE SAID TO HIM, "'YOU SHALL LOVE THE LORD YOUR GOD WITH ALL YOUR HEART, AND WITH ALL YOUR SOUL, AND WITH ALL YOUR MIND.' THIS IS THE GREAT AND FOREMOST COMMANDMENT. THE SECOND IS LIKE IT, 'YOU SHALL LOVE YOUR NEIGHBOR AS YOURSELF.' ON THESE TWO COMMANDMENTS DEPEND THE WHOLE LAW AND THE PROPHETS."
MATTHEW 22:37-40

SESSION OVERVIEW

OBJECTIVE

In this session you will help participants understand their roles and responsibilities in relationships so that they can grow together with others in Christ.

FOCUS TRUTH

In order to be a good disciple of Christ, we must assume responsibility for our own character and seek to meet the needs of others.

BRIEFING

In this session we will consider rights, responsibilities, judgment, discipline, accountability and the needs of others. The great commandment says we are to love the Lord our God with all our hearts, souls and minds, and to love our neighbor as ourselves (see Matthew 22:37-39). This sums up the whole biblical message—we are called to fall in love with God *and* with one another. A right relationship with God should lead to a right relationship with our neighbors.

GODLY RELATIONSHIPS

AND HE SAID TO HIM, "'YOU SHALL LOVE THE LORD YOUR GOD WITH ALL YOUR HEART, AND WITH ALL YOUR SOUL, AND WITH ALL YOUR MIND.' THIS IS THE GREAT AND FOREMOST COMMANDMENT. THE SECOND IS LIKE IT, 'YOU SHALL LOVE YOUR NEIGHBOR AS YOURSELF.' ON THESE TWO COMMANDMENTS DEPEND THE WHOLE LAW AND THE PROPHETS."
MATTHEW 22:37-40

WELCOME

Welcome participants and ask volunteers to share whether the Holy Spirit brought to mind anyone they had not yet forgiven for past transgressions. Then ask if anyone was brought to mind whom participants hadn't realized they needed to forgive. (Remind participants not to reveal specifics, such as names.)

Briefly review how forgiving others sets us free, and then introduce the focus of this week's session by explaining that knowing God and who we are in Christ is the foundation for Christian living. It is also the basis by which we relate to others. Share the following story:

The sign on the door read, "Puppies for Sale." So the little boy went inside to look. The man inside the pet store showed him five little puppies who were ready to leave their mother. They were about the cutest dogs the little boy had ever seen.

"How much are they?" the little boy asked.

The man replied, "Some are $50, some are more."

The little boy reached in his pocket and pulled out some change. After counting it, he said, "I have $1.47."

"Well, I'm afraid I can't sell you one of these puppies for just $1.47, little boy. You'll have to save your money and come back the next time we have more puppies for sale."

About that time, the pet store owner's wife brought out another puppy that had been hidden in the back of the store. It was smaller than the other puppies and had a bad leg. It couldn't stand up very well, and when it tried to walk, it limped very badly.

"What's wrong with that puppy?" asked the little boy. The pet store owner explained that the veterinarian had examined the puppy and had discovered that it didn't have a hip socket. It would always limp and always be lame.

"Oh, I wish I had the money to buy that puppy," the little boy exclaimed with excitement. "That is the puppy I would choose!"

"Well, that puppy is not for sale, Son. But if you really want him, I'll just give him to you. No charge."

The little boy got quite upset at the man's offer. He looked straight at the pet store owner and said, "No, I don't want you to give him to me. That little dog is worth every bit as much as the other dogs you have for sale. I'll give you $1.47 now, and I'll give you 50 cents a month until I have paid for this dog in full."

The owner of the pet store was perplexed. "You don't really want to spend your money on this little dog, Son. He's never going to be able to run and play with you like a regular puppy."

Very carefully the little boy reached down and pulled up his pant leg to reveal a badly twisted, crippled left leg, supported by a metal brace. He looked up at the pet store owner and said, "Mister, I don't run and play too good myself. I figure this little puppy is going to need someone like me who understands."

WORSHIP

Spend a few minutes worshiping the Lord through prayer, song, praise or testimonies shared by volunteers.

WORD

 The Word section is available on the Beta DVD, or you can present the information yourself in a lecture format.

GODLY RELATIONSHIPS

We have already established that grace is unwarranted favor; it cannot be earned, and it is not deserved. God has shown us grace by giving us the gift of salvation, and when we receive His grace, we discover that it really is more blessed to give than to receive. This is why it is so important to know the full gospel and all that we have received in Christ! "We love, because He first loved us" (1 John 4:19). When we know who we are in Christ, we freely give as we have freely received. We are to be merciful as He has been merciful to us (see Luke 6:36), and we are to forgive as He has forgiven us (see Ephesians 4:32).

Share the following quote by famous German pastor Johann Christoph Blumhardt:

> Neither in heaven nor on earth is it possible just to settle down comfortably through grace and do nothing and care for nobody else. If I am saved by grace, then I am a worker through grace. If I am justified by grace, then through grace I am a worker for justice. If through grace I am placed within the truth, then through grace I am a servant of truth. If through grace I have been placed within peace, then through grace I am a servant of peace for all men.[1]

RIGHTS AND RESPONSIBILITIES

Have you ever listened to a couple caught in a vicious argument? Inevitably each partner starts ripping the other's character while looking out for his or her own needs. Nobody can have good relationships with that orientation. If you want to get a biblical orientation to relationships, read the following Scripture passages:

- Romans 14:4
- Philippians 2:3-5
- 1 John 4:19-21

From these and other biblical passages, we can clearly see that we should be responsible for our own character and seek to meet the needs of others (see figure 10-A).

What would life be like if each one of us assumed our responsibility to become like Christ in our character and committed ourselves to meet the needs of everyone around us? That would truly be heaven on Earth, wouldn't it? That is what the Lord has called us to be and do (see Matthew 22:37-40). To fulfill the commandments to love God and our neighbors, we must first understand how God intended that we relate to one another.

Figure 10-A

BEING AWARE OF OUR OWN SINS

Although we look forward to seeing Jesus in His fullness someday (see 1 John 3:2), since the Fall no mortal has fully seen God. When Moses prayed "Show me Your glory" (Exodus 33:18), he was asking for a manifestation of God's presence. In answer to Moses, God placed him in the cleft of a rock and His glory passed behind him. The experience was so profound that Moses' face radiated the glory of God for days.

Isaiah had a similar experience, and when he did, he exclaimed, "Woe is me, for I am ruined! Because I am a man of unclean lips, and I live among a people of unclean lips; for my eyes have seen the King, the LORD of hosts" (Isaiah 6:5). If we, like Isaiah, were confronted with an unusual manifestation of God's presence, we would be immediately and painfully aware of our sin.

In Luke 5:3, Jesus approached Peter who had been fishing all night without success. Jesus said to him, "Put into the deep water and let down your nets for a catch" (v. 4). Peter obediently went back to the sea and started pulling in fish. He must have suddenly realized someone very special was in the boat with him, someone who could command even the fish, and he responded, "Go away from me Lord, for I am a sinful man" (v. 8).

When we are in a close relationship with God, we are more aware of our own sins and less aware of the sins of others. We should never try to be the conscience of another person. Playing the role of the Holy Spirit in another person's life won't work. The moment we try, we misdirect their struggle with God onto ourselves, and we are *not* up for that task! The Holy Spirit is the One who convicts us of our sins. The critic protests, "But I have been given the ministry of condemnation!" No, God has given us the ministry of *reconciliation* (see 2 Corinthians 5:18). The critical spirit continues, "But doesn't love expose a multitude of sins?" No. Peter wrote, "Above all, keep fervent in your love for one another, because love covers a multitude of sins" (1 Peter 4:8).

Pause for Thought
Why do you think that you as a Christian are not more inclined to follow the law of love? It is because you are so needy yourself, that you can't consider others more important than yourself?

Discipline Versus Judgment
Of course, even Christians sin, and our sin affects our relationships with God and others. Matthew 7:1-2 tells us not to judge one another, yet Galatians 6:1 tells us to carry out discipline. How can we reconcile the two?

First, we must understand that judgment is not the same as discipline. Judgment is related to character, whereas discipline is related to behavior. Discipline must be based on something seen or heard. If we observe another Christian sinning, Scripture tells us how to handle the situation. First, we are to confront the person one-on-one for the purpose of winning him or her back to the Lord. If he or she doesn't repent, we are to bring two or three others who observed the same sin. If the person still won't listen, at this point we are to tell the church (see Matthew 18:15-17). The purpose is not to condemn our brother or sister but to restore him or her to Christ.

Suppose a mother catches her son telling a lie and confronts him: "Son, what you said is not true." The boy's response might be to accuse his mother of judging him, but in truth, pointing out his sinful behavior is not judging at all. If the mother called her son a liar, however, this would cross the line from pointing out the behavior to judging her son's character.

In pointing out her son's sin, the mother is giving the boy the opportunity to acknowledge it and repent. If the mother had begun berating her son and calling him a liar (or any other derogatory term), not only would she be attacking the boy's character, but she also would be demonstrating a subtle form of rejection toward her son. The wounds left by his mother's name-calling would leave long-lasting scars on the boy.

If we could memorize and never violate Ephesians 4:29, most of the problems in our homes and churches would disappear:

> Let no unwholesome word proceed from your mouth, but only such a word as is good for edification according to the need of the moment, so that it will give grace to those who hear.

Verse 30 tells us "Do not grieve the Holy Spirit of God." It grieves God when we use words to tear one another down instead of using words to build each other up.

Pause for Thought
Have you ever had your character attacked under the disguise of discipline? How can we as Christians put correct discipline into practice in our churches and homes?

Discipline Versus Punishment
There is also a major difference between discipline and punishment. Punishment is related to the Old Testament concept of an eye for an eye. Punishment is retroactive, whereas discipline is future oriented. From Hebrews 12:5-11, we learn that God's discipline is a proof of His love. In fact, if we are not at times disciplined by God, then we are illegitimate children of God. It is important to understand, however, that God is not punishing us for our sins; that punishment fell on Christ. Our Father disciplines us so that we mature as Christians. Consider verse 11:

All discipline for the moment seems not to be joyful, but sorrowful; yet to those who have been trained by it, afterwards it yields the peaceful *fruit of righteousness* (emphasis added).

Pause for Thought
Consider the difference between punishment and discipline. Is spanking punishment or discipline? Can spanking be received as punishment and therefore not produce a harvest of righteousness? Explain.

LEARNING NOT TO BE DEFENSIVE

Although we are tempted to defend ourselves when our character is attacked by someone, we are called instead to follow the example of Christ.

And while being reviled, He did not revile in return; while suffering, He uttered no threats, but kept entrusting Himself to Him who judges righteously (1 Peter 2:23).

Before accepting Christ, we developed many methods for defending ourselves. Psychologists call these methods defense mechanisms. Now that we are alive in Christ and forgiven, we don't need to defend ourselves anymore—Christ is our defense. If a Christian is wrong, he or she doesn't have a defense; if a Christian is right, he or she doesn't *need* one! That may be hard to accept when others are passing judgement against us.

Share the following illustration:

A woman who had volunteered in a ministry at her church made an appointment with her pastor to discuss with him a list she had compiled of the pastor's good and bad points. During the appointment, the woman read through the good points (there were only two) and a whole page of bad points. As she read each point, the pastor was tempted to defend himself but instead kept quiet and allowed the woman to continue.

When the woman was through sharing the items on her list, the pastor finally spoke. "It must have taken a lot of courage to share that list with me," he said. "What do you suggest I do?"

The woman, taken aback by the pastor's response, began to cry and said, "Oh, it's not you, it's me!" This led to an important discussion that helped the pastor realize that the ministry position for which the woman was best gifted was not the ministry position she currently filled. The woman was lashing out at the pastor without realizing where her frustration really lay.

Pause for Thought
How might the situation have turned out differently if the pastor had interrupted the woman in order to defend himself against her allegations?

Nobody tears down another person from a position of strength; those who are critical of others are either doing so from a place of hurt or immaturity. If we can learn not to be defensive when our character is judged, it can lead to the opportunity to minister to others.

Shame, Guilt and Grace

Many cultures in the world are shame based. In these cultures, people are ashamed of themselves when it is perceived that there is something wrong with them. Such people lie or cover up to avoid their shame.

Legalistic churches can make people feel guilty whenever they don't measure up to the expectations of the church. Under the law, people feel guilty when they have done something wrong. Because no one can live up to everyone's expectations, this causes people in these churches to feel perpetually guilty.

Christianity is grace based. Under the grace of God, we are new creations in Christ, and we are no longer under the law. "Therefore there is now no condemnation for those who are in Christ Jesus" (Romans 8:1). To illustrate this point, think about the label "problem child." This is a popular term that is wrongly used. Would it surprise you to know that *no* parent has a problem child? That's right. If a parent had a problem child, the only way to get rid of the problem would be to get rid of the child! While a child may have problems, those problems are not who the child *is*, and therefore the problems can be solved without shaming the child.

Authority and Accountability

God has established lines of authority. Had He not done so, there would be nothing but anarchy in society. We also have a great need for accountability.

Ask participants to consider which of the following steps of authority best describes how the Lord came to them:

List A	List B
1. Authority	1. Acceptance
2. Accountability	2. Affirmation
3. Affirmation	3. Accountability
4. Acceptance	4. Authority

The list we choose reveals a lot about how we understand ministry and parenting. Paul wrote, "While we were yet sinners, Christ died for us" (Romans 5:8). Acceptance came first, and then the affirmation, "The Spirit Himself testifies with our spirit that we are children of God" (Romans 8:16).

When authority figures demand accountability without affirmation and acceptance, they will never get it. People under oppressive authority may externally comply because they are under duress, but they will never share anything intimate. Those who are accepted and affirmed, however, will voluntarily submit to an accepting and affirming person in authority.

Suppose a teenager comes home late and an overbearing dad asks in anger, "Where were you?"

Most teens would likely respond with one word: "Out!"

If the angry father continued, "What were you doing?"

He would probably receive another one-word answer: "Nothing!"

You will never read in the Gospels about Jesus saying something like "Listen here, people. You'd better shape up because I am God!" Even though He is God, and He is the ultimate authority, Jesus came to us as a gentle shepherd. After preaching the Sermon on the Mount, "The crowds were amazed at His teaching; for He was teaching them as one having authority, and not as their scribes" (Matthew 7:28-29). The same could be said for the apostle Paul when he wrote the following to the Thessalonian church:

For we never came with flattering speech, as you know, nor with a pretext for greed—God is witness—nor did we seek glory from men, either from you or from others, even though as apostles of Christ we might have asserted our authority. But we proved to be gentle among you, as a nursing mother tenderly cares for her own children. Having so fond an affection for you, we were well-pleased to impart to you not only the gospel of God but also our own lives, because you had become very dear to us (1 Thessalonians 2:5-8).

EXPRESSING OUR NEEDS

Paul wrote, "Our people must also learn to engage in good deeds to meet pressing needs, so that they will not be unfruitful" (Titus 3:14). When pressing needs are not being met, it is important that we let people know about those needs. It is prideful to let others assume that we have no needs or to refuse to share our needs with others. *Everyone* has needs, and meeting one another's needs is how we demonstrate love to one another. Just as important as making sure we express our needs is *how* we express them.

Suppose a woman whom we'll call Janice is not feeling loved or appreciated in her marriage relationship. One evening Janice approaches her husband, Joe, while the two are reading and relaxing. "You don't love me anymore, do you?" Janice asks Joe.

Perplexed by this accusation, Joe looks up from his newspaper and responds, "Of course I do!" and then goes back to reading his paper. And that's that—conversation over. Why? Because instead of stating her need, Janice judged Joe's character.

Suppose Janice had said, "Joe, I just don't feel loved right now, and I need to feel loved." By turning the "you" accusation to an "I" message, Janice expresses her need without blaming anybody. Because we are all under the command to love one another, the Holy Spirit can bring conviction to Joe, and Joe will respond differently (e.g., putting down his paper and inviting Janice to share why she is feeling unloved).

To illustrate further, what if Joe were feeling that he wasn't needed? Instead of saying, "You make me feel useless" to Janice, Joe could say, "I don't feel important in our marriage anymore." The change in the message delivery allows Janice to receive the message without blame, and she will be more open to talking with Joe to find a solution to the problem.

Pause for Thought
What are some of the needs you share in common with others?

One of Life's Little Secrets

In Acts 20:35, Jesus said, "It is more blessed to give than to receive." One of life's great compensations is that we cannot sincerely help another without helping ourselves in the process. If we want somebody to love us, we must first love someone. If we want to have friends, we must first be a friend. Whatever we measure out to others will be measured back to us.

Give, and it will be given to you. They will pour into your lap a good measure—pressed down, shaken together, and running over. For by your standard of measure it will be measured to you in return (Luke 6:38).

The following illustration makes this point:

A farmer and a baker had an arrangement to exchange a one-pound loaf of bread for one pound of butter. The arrangement went well until one day when the baker thought he could take one little pinch from each loaf-sized piece of dough to make a little more profit. *No one will know the difference*, he thought.

Soon the baker's profits began to increase just as he had thought they would. He was surprised, however, when his butter supply began to dwindle. The baker decided to go to the farmer and confront him. "You are not bringing me the same amount of butter you used to bring," the baker accused. The farmer replied, "I am doing what I've always done, good sir. For each serving of butter, I use a scale. I place your loaf of bread on one side and measure out the same amount of butter on the other until the scale is even. Then I package the butter and deliver it to you."

Let's close this session with a poem written by Mother Teresa.

ANYWAY

People are unreasonable, illogical and self-centered.
Love them anyway.
If you do good, people will accuse you
of selfish, ulterior motives.
Do good anyway.
If you are successful, you will win
false friends and true enemies.
Succeed anyway.
The good you do today will be forgotten tomorrow.
Do good anyway.
Honesty and frankness make you vulnerable.
Be honest and frank anyway.
The biggest people with the biggest ideas can be shot
down by the smallest people with the smallest minds.
Think big anyway.
People favor underdogs but follow only top dogs.
Fight for the underdog anyway.
What you spend years building
may be destroyed overnight.
Build anyway.
People really need help, but may
attack you if you help them.
Help people anyway.
Give the world the best you've got and you'll get
kicked in the teeth.
Give the world the best you've got anyway.[2]

Each of us *can* be the kind of person God created us to be in spite of others and the sad philosophies of this fallen world.

WITNESS

The following questions will help participants begin to formulate ideas for sharing their faith with others. Invite volunteers to offer suggestions for witnessing to nonbelievers, and encourage participants to write down ideas in their student guide.

1. Being an ambassador for Christ and having a positive witness are directly related to your capacity to love others. How can you be a good neighbor to those who live on your street; i.e., how can you love your neighbor as yourself?

2. What needs do your neighbors have that you could help meet?

3. How could you get to know your neighbors better so that you would have a better idea of what their needs are?

4. What needs do you share in common with your neighbors?

GROUP DISCUSSION QUESTIONS

Instruct participants to form small groups of four to six, and assign each group several questions to discuss. Allow several minutes for discussion; then bring the whole group back together, and have volunteers from each small group share their group's questions and answers.

1. What is your responsibility concerning yourself and your neighbors?

2. Why do people have a tendency to judge others and look out for their own needs?

3. If you become critical of others and unaware of your own sins, what is the problem and what can you do about it?

4. Why shouldn't you be another person's conscience? What will happen if you try to be?

5. What happens if you emphasize rights over responsibilities?

6. What is the difference between judgment and discipline?

7. What is the difference between discipline and punishment?

8. Should you be defensive if someone attacks your character? Why or why not?

9. Share a personal experience when an authority figure demanded accountability without affirmation and acceptance. How did you respond to that person? How will knowing this affect your ministry or parenting?

10. How can we share a need without its backfiring on us?

TAKING IT WITH YOU

The following information is included in the student guide and is intended for participants to use during the upcoming week. Direct participants to this section and encourage them to do the quiet-time suggestion and to consider the Big Question before the next session.

SUGGESTIONS FOR QUIET TIME

During the coming week, read Luke 6:27-42 and think about how you relate to your family, friends and neighbors. Search your heart and ask the Holy Spirit to reveal anyone from whom you should seek forgiveness. If anyone comes to mind, go to that person and state clearly what you have done wrong; then ask for forgiveness. (**Note:** Don't write a letter that can be misunderstood or used against you.)

THE BIG QUESTION

Before the next session, consider the following question:

How can you set goals for your life that are consistent with God's will?

Notes
1. Johann Christoph Blumhardt, quoted in Sherwood Eliot Wirt and Kersten Beckstrom, eds., *Living Quotations for Christians* (New York: Harper and Row, 1974), p. 97.
2. Mother Teresa, "Anyway," *Famous Quotes.com.* http://famousquotes.com/Search.php?search=Teresa&field=LastName&paint=1 (accessed October 27, 2003).

GOALS AND DESIRES

BUT THE GOAL OF OUR INSTRUCTION IS LOVE FROM A PURE
HEART AND A GOOD CONSCIENCE AND A SINCERE FAITH.
1 TIMOTHY 1:5

SESSION OVERVIEW

OBJECTIVE

In this session you will help participants understand how faith is related to our goals and desires.

FOCUS TRUTH

Nothing and no one can keep us from being the people God created us to be.

BRIEFING

God's goals for our lives are definable, defensible and achievable by faith. We must learn to differentiate between godly goals and personal desires. If we have the wrong goals, the results will be reflected in the way we live. Wrong goals can be blocked (resulting in anger), uncertain (resulting in anxiety) and impossible (leading to depression).

GOALS AND DESIRES

BUT THE GOAL OF OUR INSTRUCTION IS LOVE FROM A PURE
HEART AND A GOOD CONSCIENCE AND A SINCERE FAITH.
1 TIMOTHY 1:5

WELCOME

Welcome participants and invite a volunteer to open the meeting in prayer; then share the following parable to sow a seed for the message of this session:

There was a man who was asleep one night in his cabin when suddenly his room filled with light and the Savior appeared. The Lord told the man He had a task for him to do and showed him a large rock in front of the man's cabin. The Lord explained that the man was to push against the rock with all his might. This the man did, day after day.

For many years, the man toiled from sun up to sun down, his shoulders set squarely against the cold, massive surface of the unmoving rock, pushing with all his might. Each night the man returned to his cabin sore and worn out, feeling that whole day had been spent in vain.

Seeing that the man was showing signs of discouragement, Satan decided to enter the picture, taunting the man. "You have been pushing against that rock for a long time and it hasn't budged," Satan whispered to the man. "Why kill yourself over this? You're never going to move it!"

These taunts discouraged and disheartened the man even more. *Why kill myself over this?* he thought. *From now on, I will put in my time, giving just the minimum of effort and that will be good enough.*

One day the man decided to take his troubled thoughts to the Lord. "Lord," he said, "I have labored hard and long in Your service, putting forth all my strength to do that which You have asked. Yet, after all this time, I have not even budged that rock the tiniest bit. What is wrong? Why am I failing?"

To this the Lord responded compassionately, "My son, when long ago I asked you to serve Me and you accepted, I told you that your task was to push against the rock with all your strength, which you have done. Never once did I mention to you that I expected you to move it. Your task was to push. And now you come to Me, your strength spent, thinking that you have failed. But is that really so? Look at yourself. Your arms are strong and muscled, your back is brown, your hands are calloused from constant pressure and your legs have become massive and hard. Through opposition you have grown much and your abilities now surpass those which you used to have. No, you haven't moved the rock—but your calling was to be obedient, to push and to exercise your faith and trust in My wisdom. This you have done. And now I, My friend, will move the rock."[1]

WORSHIP

Spend a few minutes worshiping the Lord through prayer, song, praise or testimonies shared by volunteers.

WORD

 The Word section is available on the Beta DVD, or you can present the information yourself in a lecture format.

Living on the Right Path

Walking by faith is a bit like playing golf. Suppose a six-year-old boy gets his first set of golf clubs for his birthday. Each time the little fellow tees up his ball and swings away with all his might, but the farthest he can hit the ball is 60 or 70 yards. Although he would probably spray the ball all over the course, let's say he is typically 15 degrees off target. Given the length of his drive, the boy is probably still in the fairway.

As the boy grows into young adulthood (and into a bigger set of clubs), he's able to drive the ball 150 yards. Now if his drive is still 15 degrees off target, his ball is probably in the rough. Accuracy is even more important for golfers who can drive a golf ball 300 yards off the tee. The same 15-degree deviation that allowed the little boy to remain in the fairway will send the young man's longer drive soaring out of bounds.

Our Christian walk is the result of what we believe. If our faith is off, our walk will be off. If our walk is off, we need to take a good look at what we believe. For example, suppose the young golfer becomes a Christian at age 10. When he starts his walk, he's 15 degrees off, and he continues in this way throughout his life. Life eventually gets rougher, and as a grown man he finds himself completely out of bounds. He had always thought he had a good understanding of what constituted success, fulfillment and satisfaction, but now he discovers that what he had always believed about life wasn't quite true. This is often called a midlife crisis.

Walking by faith simply means functioning in daily life on the basis of what we believe. In fact, we are already walking by faith—every person alive is. The difference is in what (or whom) we believe. If what we are doing is no longer bearing any fruit, we need to change what we believe, because our misbehavior is the result of what we have chosen to believe.

Feelings Are God's Red Flags of Warning

When we are born, we begin to develop in our minds a means to succeed, find fulfillment, achieve satisfaction, have some fun, live in peace, etc. Consciously or subconsciously, we continue throughout our lifetime to formulate and adjust our plans for achieving these goals.

Sometimes our plans, well intended as they may be, are not completely in harmony with God's plans. It can be easy to wonder, *Can I ever be sure that what I believe is right? Do I have to wait until I experience some kind of midlife crisis to discover that what I believed was wrong?* The answers are yes, we can know what is right; and no, we don't have to wait until we are past our prime to find out. God has designed us in such a way that we can know on a daily basis if our belief system is properly aligned with His truth. Obviously, it must be in line with what Scripture teaches, but God has also equipped us with a feedback system that is designed to grab our attention, encouraging us to check the validity of our goals and desires. When an experience or relationship leaves us feeling angry, anxious or depressed, these emotional signposts alert us that we may be cherishing a faulty goal based on a wrong belief.

Anger Signals a Blocked Goal

When activity in a relationship or a project results in feelings of anger, it is usually because someone or something has prevented us from accomplishing what we wanted.

Pause for Thought
How do you feel when you're stuck in a traffic jam and you realize you're going to be late for an appointment?

Suppose a woman's goal is to have a loving, harmonious, happy Christian family. Who can—and will—block that goal? Every single person in the family! If that woman clings to the belief that her sense of worth is dependent on how well behaved her family is, she will crash and burn every single time her husband or child fails to live up to her image of family harmony. Eventually, her false expectations will cause her to become angry or controlling, and even feel like a defeated victim of life's circumstances, and the members of her family will be driven further away from each other.

Now suppose a pastor's goal is to reach his community for Christ. This is a wonderful desire, but if his sense of worth and success as a pastor depends on that happening, he will experience tremendous problems in his ministry. Why? Because every person in the community (including old board members) can block his goal. Pastors who believe their success is dependent on others will end up fighting with their church board or controlling members, or may just quit.

Paul wrote, "Whatever is not from faith is sin" (Romans 14:23). In other words, if what we believe is not consistent with God's Word and His will, the result is sin. An example of this is when someone or something blocks our goal—which is based on what we believe—and we respond in an outburst of anger. That outburst of anger should prompt us to reexamine both what we believe and the mental goals we have formulated to accomplish those beliefs.

Pause for Thought

How often do you get angry when you don't get your own way, or when someone or something keeps you from doing what you want to do?

Anxiety Signals an Uncertain Goal

When we feel anxious in a task or a relationship, this can be a signal that we are uncertain about our goal. For example, a teenaged girl may believe that her happiness at school depends on whether her parents allow her to attend the upcoming school dance. Not knowing how they will respond when she asks, the young girl feels anxious. If her parents tell her she can't go, she'll be angry because her goal has been blocked. But if she knows all along that there is no possibility that her parents will let her go, the girl will be depressed because her goal cannot be achieved.

Depression Signals an Impossible Goal

Depression can be the result of biochemical factors; but if there is no physical cause, then depression is often rooted in a sense of hopelessness or helplessness. This type of depression is a signal that a particular goal, no matter how spiritual or noble, may be impossible or hopeless.

Share the following illustration:

A pastor was speaking at a church on the subject of depression, and an attendee invited him and his wife to her home for dinner. The woman had been a Christian for 20 years, but her husband was not a Christian. After the pastor and his wife arrived, it didn't take long to realize that the real reason this woman had

invited them was to win her husband to Christ.

The pastor discovered later that the woman had been severely depressed for many years. Her psychiatrist insisted that her depression was endogenous—meaning internal or physical in origin—and the woman staunchly agreed; however, it became evident to the pastor that the woman's depression actually stemmed from an impossible goal: her self-worth was completely dependent on winning her family to Christ and having a Christian home. Until this goal could be met, she would always feel a failure in her life.

After a nice dinner, the pastor struck up an enjoyable conversation with the woman's husband. He was a decent man who adequately provided for the physical needs of his family. The husband listened as the pastor shared his testimony and tried to be a positive witness to the man, but the man remained convinced that he didn't need God in his life.

For over 20 years, the woman had prayed for each family member, witnessed to them and invited pastors to her home to dinner. She had said everything she could say and done everything she could do to win her family for Christ. As the futility of her efforts loomed larger, her faith faltered, her hope dimmed, and her depression grew. The resulting depression eventually affected her witness and further obliterated her goal.

Of course we *should* desire that our loved ones come to Christ, and we should pray and work to that end—but we cannot base our sense of worth as a Christian friend, parent or child on the salvation of our loved ones. We must realize that their response to our witness is beyond our ability or right to control. Witnessing is sharing our faith in the power of the Holy Spirit and leaving the results to God. *We* can't save anyone.

Sometimes depression reveals a faulty concept of God. In Psalm 13 David wrote, "How long, O LORD? Will you forget me forever? How long will You hide Your face from me? . . . How long will my enemy be exalted over me?" (vv. 1-2). Had God really forgotten David? Was He actually hiding from him? Of course not! David had a wrong concept of God and believed that He had abandoned him to the enemy. David's wrong belief about God led him to an impossible goal:

victory over his enemies without God's help. No wonder he felt depressed!

David didn't stay in the dumps, however. He evaluated his situation and realized, *I am chosen of God. I'm going to focus on what I know about Him, and not focus on my negative feelings.* As he climbed out of the pit of depression, he wrote, "But I have trusted in Your lovingkindness; my heart shall rejoice in Your salvation" (v. 5). Then he decided to make a positive expression of his will: "I will sing to the LORD, because He has dealt bountifully with me" (v. 6). He willfully moved away from his wrong concept and its accompanying depression and returned to the source of his hope.

With God all things are possible. He is the God of all hope. Turn to God when you are feeling down. "Why are you in despair, O my soul? And why are you disturbed within me? Hope in God, for I shall again praise Him, the help of my countenance and my God" (Psalm 43:5).

Pause for Thought
Depression is often the result of negative perceptions of the future, your circumstances and yourself. How can your perceptions, or beliefs, be overcome by faith in God?

WRONG RESPONSES TO THOSE WHO FRUSTRATE GOALS

Now that we understand that our goals can be blocked or uncertain, let's look at how we respond when someone or something threatens our plans. Some of us may attempt to control or manipulate people or circumstances that stand between us and our goals.

For example, let's say a young pastor who bases the success of his entire ministry on having the best youth ministry in the area wants to hire a youth pastor. Every time he takes his idea to the church board, his idea is vetoed because one of the board members feels equally adamant about hiring a music director before any other positions are filled. The young pastor, feeling that the success of his ministry is on the line, shifts into power mode and begins to lobby his cause with other board members. He doggedly seeks support for his position from other denominational leaders and looks for a way to either change the opposing board member's mind or

remove him from the board altogether. The young pastor, in his pursuit of his goal, loses sight of what is really important: his ministry.

People who cannot control those who frustrate their goals will probably respond by getting bitter, angry or resentful. Some resort to a martyr complex—as was the case in the illustration of the woman whose husband wouldn't come to Christ. Because she had been unsuccessful at bringing her husband into the Kingdom, she resigned herself to bear her cross of hopelessness and hang on until the Lord comes back.

Pause for Thought
How do you typically respond when things don't go your way? Do you try to control others or circumstances? Do you get angry, bitter or revengeful? Do you go away and sulk?

TURNING BAD GOALS INTO GOOD GOALS

If God has a goal for someone's life, can it be blocked or is its fulfillment uncertain or impossible? No God-given goal for our lives can ever be impossible, uncertain or blocked. We will never hear God say in effect, "I've called you into existence, I've made you My child, and I have something for you to do. I know you won't be able to do it, but give it your best shot." That's ludicrous! It's like saying to a child, "I want you to mow the lawn. Unfortunately, the lawn is full of rocks, the mower doesn't work, and there's no gas. But give it your best shot anyway." When an authority figures issues a command that cannot be obeyed, it undermines the authority of the leader in the minds of those who are in the position of submission.

God had a seemingly impossible goal for a young maid named Mary. An angel told her that she would bear a son while still a virgin and that her son would be the Savior of the world. When she inquired about this seemingly impossible feat, the angel simply said, "Nothing will be impossible with God" (Luke 1:37).

God does not assign goals that we can't achieve. His goals are possible, certain and achievable. We need to understand what His goals for our lives are and then say as Mary said: "Behold, the bondslave of the Lord; be it done to me according to your word" (Luke 1:38).

GOALS VERSUS DESIRES

In order to live successful lives, we need to distinguish godly goals from godly desires. This liberating distinction can spell the difference between success and failure, between inner peace and inner pain for the Christian.

- **A godly goal is any specific orientation that reflects God's purpose for our lives and does not depend on people or circumstances beyond our ability or right to control.** Whom do we have the ability and right to control? Only ourselves. The only one who can block a godly goal or render it uncertain or impossible is us. If we adopt the attitude of Mary and cooperate with God, our goal can be reached.

- **A godly desire is any specific result that depends on the cooperation of other people, or on the success of events or favorable circumstances which we have no right or ability to control.** Our successes or sense of worth cannot be based on our desires, no matter how godly our desires may be. We cannot possibly control the fulfillment of our desires. Some of them will be blocked, others will remain uncertain, and still others will eventually prove to be impossible. Let's face it: Life doesn't always go our way, and many of our desires will not be met!

We will struggle with anger, anxiety and depression when we elevate a desire to a goal in our mind. By comparison, when a desire isn't met, we only face disappointment. Life is full of disappointments, and we must learn to live with them. However, dealing with the disappointments of unmet desires is a lot easier than dealing with the anger, anxiety and depression of goals that are based on wrong beliefs.

Does God make a distinction between a goal and a desire? Yes. " 'For I have no pleasure in the death of anyone who dies,' declares the Lord GOD. 'Therefore, repent and live' " (Ezekiel 18:32). It is God's *desire* that we would all repent and live, but not all of us on Earth will. "My little children, I am writing these things to you so that you may not sin" (1 John 2:1). God's *goals*

cannot be blocked. For example, Jesus Christ will return and take us home to heaven to be with Him forever; it *will* happen. Satan will be cast into the abyss for eternity; count on it. Rewards will be distributed to the saints for their faithfulness; look forward to it. These are not desires that can be thwarted by the fickle nature of a fallen humanity. What God has determined to do, He will do.

Pause for Thought
How could differentiating between goals and desires have a tremendous effect on you and your freedom?

When we align our goals with God's goals and our desires with God's desires, we will rid ourselves of much of our anger, anxiety and depression.

GOD'S PRIMARY GOAL FOR US

God's goal for us is that we become who He created us to be. Sanctification is God's will—His goal—for our life (see 1 Thessalonians 4:3). There are distractions, diversions, disappointments, trials, temptations and traumas that come along to disrupt the process; however, the tribulations we face are actually a means of achieving the supreme goal of conforming to the image of God. Paul wrote:

> We also exult in our tribulations, knowing that tribulation brings about perseverance; and perseverance, proven character; and proven character, hope; and hope does not disappoint, because the love of God has been poured out within our hearts through the Holy Spirit who was given to us (Romans 5:3-5).

The word "exult" means "to be extremely joyful." To be under tribulation means to be under pressure, and perseverance means to remain under pressure. Persevering through tribulations results in proven character, which is God's goal for us. James offered similar counsel:

> Consider it all joy, my brethren, when you encounter various trials, knowing that the testing of your faith produces endurance. And let

endurance have its perfect result, so that you may be perfect and complete, lacking in nothing (James 1:2-4).

Share the following illustration:

Suppose a Christian woman asked her pastor for help after her husband abandoned her. What kind of hope could the pastor give her? He could say, "Don't worry, we'll win him back." Although this is a legitimate desire, it's the wrong goal. Attempts to manipulate the husband back into his marriage may be the same kind of controlling behavior that caused him to leave in the first place. The pastor would be better off telling the woman, "I will help you work through this crisis (perseverance) so that you become the person God wants you to be (proven character). If you haven't committed yourself to be the wife and mother God has called you to be, would you do that now? You can't change your husband, but you can change yourself. Even if he doesn't come back, you can come through this crisis with proven character; and that is where your hope lies."

The woman may rightly counter with, "What if the problem was 90 percent his?" Unfortunately, the wife has no control over that, but in committing to change herself she is responsibly dealing with what she *can* control. Her transformation may be just the motivation her husband needs to change himself and restore their relationship.

Trials and tribulations reveal wrong goals, but they can also be the catalysts for achieving God's ultimate goal for our lives—our sanctification. Sanctification is the process of conforming to His image. It's during these times of pressure that our emotions raise their warning flags, signaling blocked, uncertain or impossible goals that are based on our desires instead of on God's goal of proven character.

Too often, defeated spouses try to solve their unhappy, or hopeless, marriage by changing partners, only to find that second marriages have an even higher rate of failing. Some people feel their jobs or churches are hopeless and leave only to discover that their new job or church is just as hopeless. Rather than controlling

and changing the one thing they can—themselves—these people are running away from what they perceive as the problem, only to find out that the problem follows them.

Share Neil Anderson's experience with how powerful the truth of this message is:

A suit salesman heard this message about desires and goals, and it changed his life. Some time after hearing the message, he approached me and shared his story.

The man had been an angry salesman. His boss had even had to call him aside a number of times because of his temper. The salesman had set a personal goal for himself to sell a certain number of suits each week, and he would hound customers and manipulate sales—anything he needed to do to reach his self-imposed weekly quota.

After hearing the truth in this message, the man realized that he had set the wrong goal for himself. He decided to become the salesman God had called him to be. He set aside his weekly quota and changed his approach. It had such an effect on the man in just one week that his boss came to him asking if he was okay.

Because the man sought God's will and not his own, the anger dissipated, and he started to consider each customer as more important than he was (see Philippians 2:3-5). To his surprise, he sold more suits than he ever had before.

Pause for Thought
Is it liberating or convicting to know that nothing can keep you from being the person God created you to be? Why?

Is there a way to conform to God's image that does not involve having to endure painful tribulations? Every Christian has probably looked for one, but the difficult times of testing bring about the maturity that makes life meaningful. We do need occasional mountaintop experiences, but the fertile soil for growth is always down in the valleys, not at the top of the mountain. Paul wrote, "The goal of our instruction is love" (1 Timothy 1:5).

Love, or agape, is the character of God because "God is love" (1 John 4:8). When we make godly character our primary goal, then the fruit of the Spirit is love (instead of hatred), joy (instead of depression), peace (instead of anxiety) and patience (instead of anger).

Share the following poem from an unknown author, which expresses so well the message of this session.

"Disappointments—His appointment,"
Change one letter, then I see
That the thwarting of my purpose
Is God's better choice for me.
His appointment must be blessing,
Tho' it may come in disguise,
For the end from the beginning
Open to His wisdom lies.

"Disappointment—His appointment,"
No good will He withhold,
From denials oft we gather
treasures of His love untold.
Well He knows each broken purpose
Leads to fuller, deeper trust,
And the end of all His dealings
Proves our God is wise and just.

"Disappointments—His appointment,"
Lord, I take it, then, as such,
Like clay in hands of a potter,
Yielding wholly to Thy touch.
My life's plan is Thy molding;
Not one single choice be mine;
Let me answer, unrepining
"Father, not my will, but Thine."

WITNESS

The following question will help participants begin to formulate ideas for sharing their faith with others. Invite volunteers to offer suggestions for witnessing to nonbelievers, and encourage participants to write down ideas in their student guide.

How can distinguishing between goals and desires make you a better witness?

GROUP DISCUSSION QUESTIONS

Instruct participants to form small groups of four to six, and assign each group several questions to discuss. Allow several minutes for discussion; then bring the whole group back together, and have volunteers from each small group share their group's questions and answers.

1. If goals and desires are something you adopt in your own mind, how can you know emotionally if you are in the center of God's will?

2. How does the world typically respond to blocked goals? What has been your typical response?

3. Why is a manipulator or controller insecure? What false beliefs is such a person harboring?

4. What is God's primary goal for your life? Why can't that goal be blocked?

5. How does the fruit of the Spirit demonstrate the antithesis of false goals?

6. How does a Christian establish a legitimate sense of worth?

7. How can you live so that you never stumble, and if you aren't living that way, what should you do about it?

TAKING IT WITH YOU

The following information is included in the student guide and is intended for participants to use during the upcoming week. Direct participants to this section and encourage them to do the quiet-time suggestion and to consider the Big Question before the next session.

SUGGESTION FOR QUIET TIME

This coming week, take the time to evaluate your faith by completing the following Faith Appraisal. Circle the number that best describes your answer to each question; then complete the sentence that follows each question. (**Note:** You will *not* be asked to share your results with the group. This is a self-appraisal to help you evaluate your own faith.)

	Low				**High**
1. How successful am I?	1	2	3	4	5

I would be more successful if . . .

2. How significant am I? 1 2 3 4 5
I would be more significant if . . .

3. How fulfilled am I? 1 2 3 4 5
I would be more fulfilled if . . .

4. How satisfied am I? 1 2 3 4 5
I would be more satisfied if . . .

5. How happy am I? 1 2 3 4 5
I would be happier if . . .

6. How much fun am I having? 1 2 3 4 5
I would have more fun if . . .

7. How secure am I? 1 2 3 4 5
I would be more secure if . . .

8. How peaceful am I? 1 2 3 4 5
I would have more peace if . . .

THE BIG QUESTION

Before the next session, consider the following question:

> If you discover that your goals are not the same as God's goals for your life, what will you need to do to change your focus?

Note
1. Jim Burns and Mike DeVries, *Intense Illustrations* (Ventura, CA: Gospel Light, 2002), pp. 94-95.

LIVING ON THE RIGHT PATH

NOT THAT I SPEAK FROM WANT, FOR I HAVE LEARNED TO BE CONTENT IN WHATEVER CIRCUMSTANCES I AM. I KNOW HOW TO GET ALONG WITH HUMBLE MEANS, AND I ALSO KNOW HOW TO LIVE IN PROSPERITY; IN ANY AND EVERY CIRCUMSTANCE I HAVE LEARNED THE SECRET OF BEING FILLED AND GOING HUNGRY, BOTH OF HAVING ABUNDANCE AND SUFFERING NEED. I CAN DO ALL THINGS THROUGH HIM WHO STRENGTHENS ME.
PHILIPPIANS 4:11-13

SESSION OVERVIEW

OBJECTIVE

In this final session of the Beta course you will help participants evaluate their lives in light of God's Word and change what they believe so that they can begin down the path of sanctification.

FOCUS TRUTH

Each of us lives by faith. We must examine what we believe and renew our minds to the truth of God's Word if we are going to be successful, fulfilled, satisfied and content.

BRIEFING

In this last session we will examine what we believe in light of God's Word concerning eight aspects of our personal life. If participants completed the Faith Appraisal from last week's session, their answers reflect what they presently believe and how they are living accordingly.

Note:
This last session of the Beta course does not contain any Pause for Thought messages. Instead, consider how each of the issues addressed can be applied by the group participants.

LIVING ON THE RIGHT PATH

NOT THAT I SPEAK FROM WANT, FOR I HAVE LEARNED TO BE CONTENT IN WHATEVER CIRCUMSTANCES I AM. I KNOW HOW TO GET ALONG WITH HUMBLE MEANS, AND I ALSO KNOW HOW TO LIVE IN PROSPERITY; IN ANY AND EVERY CIRCUMSTANCE I HAVE LEARNED THE SECRET OF BEING FILLED AND GOING HUNGRY, BOTH OF HAVING ABUNDANCE AND SUFFERING NEED. I CAN DO ALL THINGS THROUGH HIM WHO STRENGTHENS ME.

PHILIPPIANS 4:11-13

WELCOME

Welcome participants and open the meeting in prayer. Give a brief review of the main message from session 11—that no one and nothing can keep us from being who God created us to be—and then share the following illustration:

I am part of the "Fellowship of the Unashamed"—I have "Holy Spirit Power." The die has been cast, and I've stepped over the line. The decision has been made: I am a disciple of His. I won't look back, let up, slow down, back away or be still. My past is redeemed, my present makes sense and my future is secure. I am finished with low living, sight walking, small planning, smooth knees, colorless dreams, tame visions, mundane talking, chintzy giving and dwarfed goals!

I no longer need preeminence, prosperity, position, promotions, plaudits or popularity. I don't have to be right, first, tops, recognized, praised, regarded or rewarded. I now live by presence, learn by faith, love by patience, lift by prayer and labor by power.

My face is set; my gait is fast; my goal is heaven; my road is narrow; my way is rough; my companions few; my guide reliable; my mission clear. I cannot be bought, compromised, detoured, lured away, turned back, diluted or delayed. I will not flinch in the face of sacrifice, hesitate in the presence of adversity, negotiate at the table of the enemy, ponder at the pool of popularity or meander in the maze of mediocrity.

I won't give up, shut up, let up or burn up till I've preached up, prayed up, paid up, stored up and stayed up for the cause of Christ.

I am a disciple of Jesus. I must go till He comes, give till I drop, preach till all know and work till He stops.

And when He comes to get His own, He'll have no problems recognizing me. My colors will be clear.[1]

WORSHIP

Spend a few minutes worshiping the Lord through prayer, song, praise or testimonies shared by volunteers.

WORD

 The Word section is available on the Beta DVD, or you can present the information yourself in a lecture format.

We live by faith, according to what we believe. Assuming that our basic physiological needs of food, shelter and safety are met, we are motivated to live successful, significant, fulfilled, satisfied, happy, fun, secure and peaceful lives. That is reasonable—after all, God has not called us to be insecure, insignificant or unfulfilled. We probably don't have the same definition that God does for the eight qualities of life listed in the Faith Appraisal, so we are not living up to our God-given potential. In this last session, we're going to consider each one of these qualities.

GOD'S GUIDELINES FOR THE WALK OF FAITH

Success (Key Concept: Goals)

Success is accepting God's goals for our lives and, by His grace, becoming what He has called us to be (see Joshua 1:7-8; 2 Peter 1:3-10; 3 John 2).

A troubled woman named Mattie had many moral lapses and made an appointment to see her pastor. When they met, she quoted the first part of 3 John 2: "Beloved, I pray that in all respects you may prosper and be in good health" and then asked, "If God has promised prosperity, success and good health, why am I not experiencing it?" Mattie had her answer, but she had failed to read it in the remainder of the verse: "Just as your soul prospers." She was experiencing about as much success as her soul was experiencing.

We can be complete failures in the eyes of the world and still be successful in the eyes of God. Conversely, we can be huge successes in the world and be failures for eternity.

When we have difficulty reaching our goals, this may be due to our not working on the *right* goals. Success is related to goals, and each of us has different goals. However, 2 Peter 1:3-10 tells us that there is one universal goal for everyone. Read it aloud.

Notice that God's goal begins with who we are on the basis of what He has already done for us. He has given us "life and godliness" (v. 3). We are forgiven and on the path of sanctification (i.e., conforming to the image of God). We are already partakers of the divine nature and have already escaped sin's corruption. What a great start!

Our primary job, then, is to diligently adopt God's character goals—moral excellence, knowledge, self-control, perseverance, godliness, brotherly kindness and Christian love—and apply them to our lives each day. We have been promised that as these qualities increase in our lives through practice, we will be useful and fruitful and we will never stumble. Focusing on God's goals will lead us to ultimate success *in God's terms*. That is a legitimate basis for our true sense of worth and success.

Notice also that Peter does not say that these talents, intelligence and gifts are not equally distributed to all believers. Our identity and sense of worth are based on our identity in Christ and our growth in character, which are equally accessible to every Christian. Christians who are not committed to God's goals for character have forgotten their purification from former sins; they have forgotten who they are in Christ. The woman named Mattie was an example of one such Christian.

Another helpful perspective of success is seen in Joshua's experience of leading Israel into the Promised Land.

> Only be strong and very courageous; be careful to do according to all the law which Moses My servant commanded you; do not turn from it to the right or to the left, so that you may have success wherever you go. This book of the law shall not depart from your mouth, but you shall meditate on it day and night, so that you may be careful to do according to all that is written in it; for then you will make your way prosperous, and then you will have success (Joshua 1:7-8).

Joshua's success hinged not on other people or circumstances; instead, his success depended entirely on living according to God's Word. He had only to listen to God and do what God said. This sounds simple enough, but God immediately put Joshua to the test by giving him a rather unorthodox battle plan for conquering Jericho—marching around the city for seven days and then blowing a horn wasn't exactly an orthodox military tactic! However, regardless of how foolish God's plan may have seemed to Joshua, his success could only be found through his obedience to the Lord. Success is accepting God's goals for our lives and *by His grace* becoming what He has called us to be.

Significance (Key Concept: Time)

What is forgotten in the passing of time is of little significance. What is remembered for eternity is of greatest significance (see Acts 5:33-40; 1 Corinthians 3:13; 1 Timothy 4:7-8).

Significance is a time concept. Paul wrote to the Corinthians: "If any man's work . . . remains, he will receive a reward" (1 Corinthians 3:14). He instructed Timothy to discipline himself "for the purpose of godliness . . . since it holds promise for the present life and also for the life to come" (1 Timothy 4:7-8).

If our desire is to increase our significance, we must be willing to focus our energies on significant activities that will remain for eternity. Think about what the world considers significant and how it compares to God's Word. The team who wins the Super Bowl or the World Series this year may capture the headlines for a time, but does it really matter who won 25 years ago? We keep records and build memorials, but within a generation the deeds have been outdone and over time the memories fade.

Unlike the things of this world that are bound to fade, as Christians we are called to do Kingdom work that will last forever. It may feel to the Sunday School teacher that teaching third graders every Sunday is not so significant; however, teaching the truth every week to impressionable young children will help equip them to make choices in their lives that will have eternal consequences. Even the nursery staff is contributing to lasting Kingdom work. Because of the nursery staff, parents are free to worship God and receive instruction that will help them raise their families for the Kingdom. The bottom line is that not one child of God is insignificant; therefore, there are no insignificant tasks in His kingdom!

Fulfillment (Key Concept: Role Preference)

Fulfillment is discovering our own uniqueness in Christ and using our gifts to build others up and glorify the Lord (see Matthew 25:14-30; Romans 12:1-18; 2 Timothy 4:5).

Fulfillment is achieved when we bloom where we're planted. "As each one has received a special gift, employ it in serving one another" (1 Peter 4:10).

Share Neil Anderson's experience:

I received the Lord while I was working as an aerospace engineer, and I knew that God wanted me to be an ambassador for Christ on the job, so I decided to start a Bible-study breakfast in the bowling alley next door to where I worked. The announcement about the Bible study had only been posted in the office about an hour before a Jewish fellow pulled it off the wall and brought it to me. "You can't bring Jesus in here," he objected.

"I can't do otherwise," I responded. "Every day that I walk in here Jesus comes in with me." As you can imagine, the not-yet Christian was less than impressed with my response!

One of the men who found Christ through the Bible study became a powerful witness at the plant, passing out tracts everywhere he went; and when I left that aerospace firm to enter seminary, this new convert took over the Bible study.

A few months after I left the firm, I visited my friends during one of the breakfast Bible studies. "Do you remember the Jewish fellow?" the leader asked.

"Sure, I remember him." How could I not remember his brash opposition to the Bible study?

"Well, he got sick and almost died, and I went to the hospital to visit him every night. I thought you would like to know that I led him to the Lord."

It all began when a new believer started a simple Bible study in the place where he worked in order to "do the work of an evangelist, fulfill your ministry" (2 Timothy 4:5).

God has a unique place of ministry for each of us, and it is important to our sense of fulfillment that we realize our calling in life. The key is discovering the roles we occupy in which we cannot be replaced—and then decide to be what God wants us to be in those roles. For example, of the 6 billion people in the world, each one of us has a unique role in our family. Whether we are the husband, wife, father, mother or child, God has specially planted us to serve Him by serving our family in that role.

Furthermore, we are uniquely positioned where we live and where we work; these are our mission fields and we are the workers God has appointed for the harvest there. Our greatest fulfillment will come from accepting and occupying God's unique place for us to the best of our abilities. Fulfillment cannot be found in the world—we must find our fulfillment in the kingdom of God by deciding to be ambassadors for Christ in the world (see 2 Corinthians 5:20).

Satisfaction (Key Concept: Quality)

Satisfaction is living righteously and seeking to raise the quality of the relationships, services and products with which we are involved (see Proverbs 18:24; Matthew 5:6; 2 Timothy 4:7).

Jesus said, "Blessed are those who hunger and thirst for righteousness, for they shall be satisfied" (Matthew 5:6). If we believe what Jesus said, we should be hungering and thirsting after righteousness. If we aren't doing this, we don't really believe it.

Satisfaction is a quality issue, not a quantity issue. When asked to identify at what point they became dissatisfied with something, people will typically respond by sharing a time when the quality of a relationship, service or work diminished. Greater satisfaction is achieved from doing a few things well rather than from doing many things in a haphazard or hasty manner.

The key to personal satisfaction is not found in broadening the scope of our activities but in deepening them through a commitment to quality. The same is true with relationships, including friendships. Dissatisfaction in a relationship can be an indicator that we have spread ourselves too thin. King Solomon wrote, "A man of too many friends comes to ruin, but there is a friend who sticks closer than a brother" (Proverbs 18:24).

Even in friendships, quality—not quantity—is the key, and that is what our Lord modeled for us. He taught the multitudes, and He equipped 70 for ministry, but He invested most of His time in just 12 disciples. Out of those 12, He selected three—Peter, James and John—to be with Him on the Mount of Transfiguration, on the Mount of Olives and in the Garden of Gethsemane. While suffering on the cross, Jesus committed the care of His mother, Mary, to John. That's a quality relationship, and we all need the satisfaction that quality relationships bring.

Happiness (Key Concept: Wanting What You Have)

Happiness is being thankful for what we do have rather than focusing on what we don't have (see Philippians 4:12; 1 Thessalonians 5:18; 1 Timothy 6:6-8).

The world's concept of happiness is having what we want. Advertisers tell us that we need a flashier car, a sexier cologne, a bigger house—or any number of items that are better, faster or easier to use than what we already have. We watch the commercials and read the ads, and we become antsy to get all the latest fashions, fads and fancy doodads. We have been programmed by the world to think that we will be happy if only we have whatever it is that we don't already have.

True happiness is summed up in this simple phrase: "Happy are those who want what they have." Paul knew this and shared it in 1 Timothy 6:6-8:

> But godliness actually is a means of great gain when accompanied by contentment. For we have brought nothing into the world, so we cannot take anything out of it either. If we have food and covering, with these we shall be content.

As Christians we already have everything we need to make us happy forever: We have Jesus Christ, and through Him we have eternal life. We are loved by a heavenly Father who has promised to supply all our needs. No wonder the Bible repeatedly commands us to be thankful (see 1 Thessalonians 5:18)!

Fun (Key Concept: Uninhibited Spontaneity)

The secret to fun is removing unbiblical blocks such as keeping up appearances (see 2 Samuel 6:20-22; Romans 14:22; Galatians 1:10; 5:1).

Fun is uninhibited spontaneity. Some people abuse alcohol and drugs to remove their inhibitions; however, this is the wrong approach. To enjoy godly spontaneity, we must remove unscriptural inhibitors. Chief among these is our fleshly tendency to want to keep up appearances.

We don't want to look out of place or be thought less of by others, so we stifle our spontaneity with a form of false decorum. That's "people pleasing," and Paul wrote that anyone who lives to please people isn't serving Christ (see Galatians 1:10). Their joyless cry is, "What will people say?" The liberated in Christ respond, "Who cares what people say? I care what God says, and I stopped playing for the grandstand a long time ago when I started playing for the coach."

King David was full of uninhibited joy. He was so happy about returning the ark to Jerusalem that he leapt and danced before the Lord in celebration (see 1 Samuel 6:14). David knew there was joy in the presence of God. David's wife, Michal, however, was more concerned with appearances. She thought his behavior had been unbecoming to a king. David's reply to her was that he had not been dancing for her or anyone else; he had been dancing before the Lord, and he would continue to do so whether she liked it or not!

(See 2 Samuel 6:21). In the end, it was Michal who was judged by God, not David (see 2 Samuel 6:23). It is a lot more fun to please the Lord than to try to please people.

Security (Key Concept: Relating to the Eternal)

Insecurity comes when we depend on things that will pass away rather than on things that will last forever (see John 10:27-29; Romans 8:31-39; Ephesians 1:13-14).

Insecurity is depending on temporal things over which we have no right or ability to control. Insecurity is a global problem. With an exploding world population and decreasing natural resources, there are going to be some tough days ahead for this fallen world; it doesn't take a genius to figure that out. Our security can only be found in the eternal life of Christ. Jesus said that no one can snatch us out of His hand (see John 10:27-29), and Paul declared that nothing can separate us from the love of God in Christ (see Romans 8:35-39). We are sealed "in Him" by the Holy Spirit (Ephesians 1:13-14). There is no better security than that. Every "thing" we now have will someday be gone. Jim Elliot said, "He is no fool to give up that which he cannot keep in order to gain that which he cannot lose."[2]

> But whatever things were gain to me, those things I have counted as loss for the sake of Christ. More than that, I count all things to be loss in view of the surpassing value of knowing Christ Jesus my Lord, for whom I have suffered the loss of all things, and count them but rubbish so that I may gain Christ (Philippians 3:7-8).

Peace (Key Concept: Establishing Internal Order)

The peace of God is internal, not external (see Isaiah 32:17; Jeremiah 6:14; John 14:27; Philippians 4:6-7).

Peace on Earth and good will toward men—that is a great desire, but the wrong goal. Nobody can guarantee external peace because nobody can control people or circumstances. Throughout history nations have signed and broken peace treaties with frightening regularity. One group of peace marchers confronts a group of activists, and they end up beating each other over the head with their placards. Husbands and wives lament to themselves that there would be peace in their home if only their spouse would shape up.

Peace *with* God is something we already have (see Romans 5:1). The peace *of* God is something we must appropriate daily in our inner person. There are a lot of things that can disrupt our external world because we can't control all of our circumstances and relationships. But we *can* control the inner world of our thoughts and emotions by allowing the peace of God to rule in our hearts on a daily basis.

Nothing will happen to us today that we cannot handle with God. Personal worship, prayer and interaction with God's Word enable us to experience His peace (see Philippians 4:6-7; Colossians 3:15-16).

The nonbeliever will say, "Well, I suppose that's true, but I still believe . . ." Which will that person live by: what he or she mentally acknowledges as true or what he or she still believes? Always the latter—*always!* Walking by faith is simply choosing to believe that what God says is true and living accordingly by the power of the Holy Spirit. May the good Lord enable each of us to do so.

WITNESS

The following question will help participants begin to formulate ideas for sharing their faith with others. Invite volunteers to offer suggestions for witnessing to nonbelievers, and encourage participants to write down ideas in their student guide.

How can you be a good ambassador for Christ?

GROUP DISCUSSION QUESTIONS

Instruct participants to form small groups of four to six, and assign each group several questions to discuss. Allow several minutes for discussion; then bring the whole group back together, and have volunteers from each small group share their group's questions and answers.

1. How can a successful politician, businessperson or scientist live consistently with God's Word?

2. On what does your success as a Christian depend?

3. What does the world call "significant" that in light of eternity is really insignificant?

4. How can you live a more fulfilled life?

5. Can anything the flesh craves ever be satisfying?

   What satisfies and continues to satisfy?

6. How can you truly be happy in this world?

7. How can you experience the joy of the Lord and make your Christian experience more fun?

8. What causes you to feel insecure?

   How can you be more secure?

9. How do goals and desires relate to the possibility of experiencing peace?

10. What kind of peace can you have and how do you get it?

Notes
 1. Source unknown.
 2. Jim Elliot, *The Journals of Jim Elliot*, ed. Elisabeth Elliot (Old Tappan, NJ: Fleming H. Revell Co., 1978), p. 174.

BOOKS AND RESOURCES
BY DR. NEIL T. ANDERSON

CORE MESSAGE AND MATERIALS

The Bondage Breaker with study guide, audio book (Harvest House Publishers, 2000)—with well over 1 million copies in print, this book explains spiritual warfare, what our protection is, ways that we are vulnerable and how we can live a liberated life in Christ.

Breaking Through to Spiritual Maturity (Regal Books, 2000)—this curriculum teaches the basic message of Freedom in Christ Ministries.

Discipleship Counseling and videocassettes (Regal Books, 2003)—combines the concepts of discipleship and counseling and the practical integration of theology and psychology for helping Christians resolve their personal and spiritual conflicts through repentance.

The Steps to Freedom in Christ and interactive videocassette (Regal Books, 2000)—this discipleship counseling tool helps Christians resolve their personal and spiritual conflicts.

Victory over the Darkness and study guide, audiobook, and videocassettes (Regal Books, 2000)—with well over 1 million copies in print, this core book explains who you are in Christ, how you walk by faith, how your mind and emotions function, and how to relate to one another in Christ.

SPECIALIZED BOOKS

The Biblical Guide to Alternative Medicine with Dr. Michael Jacobson (Regal Books, 2003)—develops a grid by which you can evaluate medical practices. It applies the grid to the world's most recognized philosophies of medicine and health.

Blessed Are the Peacemakers with Dr. Charles Mylander (Regal Books, 2002)—explains the ministry of reconciliation and gives practical steps for being reconciled with others.

Breaking the Strongholds of Legalism with Rich Miller and Paul Travis (Harvest House Publishers, 2003)—an exposure and explanation of legalism and how to overcome it.

The Christ-Centered Marriage with Dr. Charles Mylander (Regal Books, 1997)—explains God's divine plan for marriage and the steps that couples can take to resolve their difficulties.

Christ-Centered Therapy with Dr. Terry and Julie Zuehlke (Zondervan Publishing House, 2000)—a textbook explaining the practical integration of theology and psychology for professional counselors.

Daily in Christ with Joanne Anderson (Harvest House Publishers, 2000)—this popular daily devotional is being used by thousands of Internet subscribers every day.

Finding Hope Again with Hal Baumchen (Regal Books, 1999)—explains depression and how to overcome it.

Freedom from Addiction with Mike and Julia Quarles (Regal Books, 1997)—using Mike's testimony, this book explains the nature of chemical addictions and how to overcome them in Christ.

Freedom from Fear with Rich Miller (Harvest House Publishers, 1999)—explains anxiety disorders and how to overcome them.

Freedom in Christ Bible (Zondervan Publishing House, 2002)—a one-year discipleship study with notes in the Bible.

Getting Anger Under Control with Rich Miller (Harvest House Publishers, 1999)—explains the basis for anger and how to control it.

God's Power at Work in You with Dr. Robert L. Saucy (Harvest House Publishers, 2001)—a thorough analysis of sanctification and practical instruction on how we grow in Christ.

Leading Teens to Freedom in Christ with Rich Miller (Regal Books, 1997)—this discipleship counseling book focuses on teenagers, their problems and how to solve them.

One Day at a Time with Mike and Julia Quarles (Regal Books, 2000)—this devotional helps those who struggle with addictive behaviors and how to discover the grace of God on a daily basis.

Released from Bondage with Dr. Fernando Garzon and Judith E. King (Thomas Nelson, 2002)—contains personal accounts of bondage and explanatory notes showing how people found their freedom in Christ, and how the message of Freedom in Christ can be applied to therapy with research results.

The Seduction of Our Children with Steve Russo (Harvest House Publishers, 1991)—explains what teenagers are experiencing and how parents can be equipped to help them.

Setting Your Church Free with Dr. Charles Mylander (Regal Books, 1994)—this book on Christian leadership also explains corporate bondage and how it can be resolved in Christ.

Spiritual Protection for Your Children with Peter and Sue Vander Hook (Regal Books, 1996)—using the Vander Hook's experience, this book explains how parents can help their children.

A Way of Escape with Russ Rummer (Harvest House Publishers, 1998)—explains sexual strongholds and how they can be torn down in Christ.

Who I Am in Christ (Regal Books, 2001)—describes in 36 short chapters who you are in Christ and how He meets your deepest needs.

VICTORY OVER THE DARKNESS SERIES

Overcoming Negative Self-Image with Dave Park (Regal Books, 2003)

Overcoming Addictive Behavior with Mike Quarles (Regal Books, 2003)

Overcoming Depression with Joanne Anderson (Regal Books, 2004)

Overcoming Doubt (Regal Books, 2004)

BONDAGE BREAKER SERIES

Finding Freedom in a Sex-Obsessed World (Harvest House Publishers, 2004)

Finding God's Will in Spiritually Deceptive Times (Harvest House Publishers, 2003)

Praying by the Power of the Spirit (Harvest House Publishers, 2003)

YOUTH BOOKS

Awesome God with Rich Miller (Harvest House Publishers, 1996)

The Bondage Breaker—Youth Edition with Dave Park (Harvest House Publishers, 2001)

Extreme Faith with Dave Park (Harvest House Publishers, 1996)

Higher Ground with Dave Park and Dr. Robert L. Saucy (1999)*

Purity Under Pressure with Dave Park (Harvest House Publishers, 1995)

Radical Image with Dave Park and Dr. Robert L. Saucy (Harvest House Publishers, 1998)*

Real Life with Dave Park (Harvest House Publishers, 2000)*

Reality Check with Rich Miller (Harvest House Publishers, 1996)

Righteous Pursuit with Dave Park (Harvest House Publishers, 2000)

Stomping Out Depression with Dave Park (Harvest House Publishers, 2001)

Stomping Out Fear with Dave Park and Rich Miller (Harvest House Publishers, 2003)

Stomping Out the Darkness with Dave Park (Regal Books, 1999)

Ultimate Love with Dave Park (Harvest House Publishers, 1996)

*Available from Freedom in Christ Ministries only

FREEDOM IN CHRIST MINISTRIES

9051 Executive Park Drive, Suite 503
Knoxville, Tennessee 37923
Phone: 865-342-4000
Fax: 865-342-4001
E-Mail: info@ficm.org
Website: http://www.ficm.org

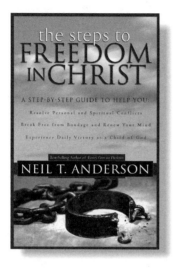
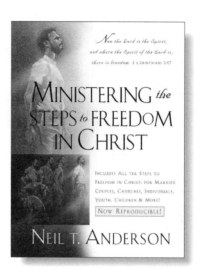
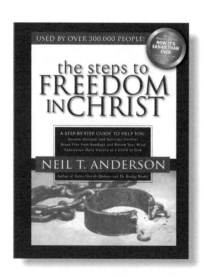
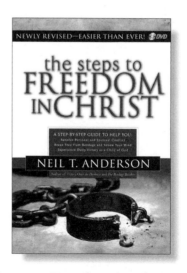